Full-Contact Living

Preparing for the Martial Arts of Everyday Life!

Full-Contact Living

Preparing for the Martial Arts of Everyday Life!

Rodney King

Rodney King

2015

First Printing: 2015

ISBN 978-0-620-64659-8

For information, contact:

rodney@embodiedmba.com

Printed in the United States of America.

Visit:www.fullcontactliving.org

Dedication

To my wife Louise, for listening to me endlessly talk about my dreams, and believing in my vision of teaching martial arts that transcends the fight. To my boys, Egan and Tobynn, for ensuring that I practice daily the lessons that are held within in this book. You rock!

Acknowledgements

Thank you to my friend Andrew Robertson for the amazing art in this book. To find out more about Andy's incredible work go to: www.glyph.co.za

Contents

Foreword

Christian de Quincey

One evening, a few years ago now, I got an email from someone I didn't know. He had found one of my books in a local bookstore in Johannesburg, and *just had to connect.* Apparently, he had randomly flipped open to a section where I had written about the mysterious mind-body connection, and he was astounded to find language that exactly matched what he had learned from direct embodied experience over the years as a martial artist.

That was how I first "met" Rodney King, martial artist coach extraordinaire and internationally successful entrepreneur. I immediately wrote back, and so began our regular correspondence, and a deep and lasting friendship.

At first, Rodney wanted me to mentor him in the ideas and language of "Consciousness Studies," with special focus on the mind-body relationship—my field of scholarship for many years. I agreed, and so we moved to the next level, meeting weekly via Skype. The time difference between where I live (California) and his home (Johannesburg) meant the most convenient hour for us to talk was around 7:00 AM his time, 9:00 PM my time, a day earlier. It worked out just fine. For more than a year, Rodney and I explored the mysteries of mind-body through books, email exchanges, and websites. Rodney wrote essays about what he had learned, and offered insights on how he would apply some of my ideas about the mind-body connection to his martial arts/leadership coaching practice—a great way to "embody" the new language and terminology he had now discovered. I gave feedback, and our rich dialogues deepened as we explored a common passion for integrating mind and body—conceptually and somatically through self-expressive action.

Martial Artist Meets Philosopher

About a year later, Rodney (a world-class martial arts coach) and I (author and philosopher) decided to work together—in archetypal terms: Warrior meets Sage. We co-authored a book, *Embodied-Mind Performance,* which summarized and clarified the philosophical foundations for Crazy Monkey Defense, a unique form of martial arts created by Rodney, and now offered in fifteen countries around the world.

Based on our collaboration, we decided to host a series of "Embodied-Mind" workshops, starting in South Africa, later in the U.S. and Australia. So I flew to Johannesburg, my first visit to Southern Africa. I finally got to meet Rodney in person; it felt like reuniting with a brother, and time to switch roles. I now became his student as he taught me the fundamentals of his style of martial arts. This was a perfect opportunity for me to put into practice, *literally,* ideas I had been thinking and writing about for decades. Whereas Rodney came to me for words to put to consciousness, and mind-body interaction, I came to him for the pragmatic embodied experience of putting mind-body unity into action.

Like many people interested in exploring consciousness, I have meditated for many years—a worthy practice for learning to observe the flux and flow of the mind. I have written and lectured on the value of mindfulness—being fully present and aware of whatever is happening in your mind-body *as it happens.*

Sparring with Rodney on the mat in his home studio, however, I got a lesson in the difference between mindfulness sitting on a cushion and *mindfulness-in-action.* It's one thing to achieve a level of peaceful, non-judgmental, non-reactive self-observation during meditation; it is altogether something else to maintain such presence of mind when someone (stronger and bigger than you) is throwing punches at your face. Even though I knew he had no intention of hurting me, my body still tensed and flinched as his glove glanced across my cheek. Here, I had an opportunity to face my fears and pay closer attention to how my mind reacts to what happens in my body, and how my body reacts to thoughts and emotions zipping through my mind.

This is what Rodney calls "the mental game"—developing a disciplined presence of mind in the face of *whatever* challenges rise before you. This could be while sparring in a martial arts dojo, negotiating an important business deal in a corporate boardroom, pursuing law-enforcement on city streets, or fighting on a modern battlefield.

While Rodney pays a great deal of attention to the power of the mind in martial arts (and in everyday life), this is never at the expense of honoring the power and natural intelligence of the body itself. Whereas most modern martial artists and coaches focus on training the *body,* Rodney's approach emphasizes disciplined mental training, viewing it just as, if not more, crucial for achieving peak performance—*in anything.*

Rodney is committed to martial arts as a way of life—a way of life that aims at holistic self-development and enrichment. This doesn't just involve training aimed at achieving a degree of mastery in a particular skill, embodied or mental, but also crucially involves attending to the quality of our *relationships*—with other people and with the wider world around us.

As you will discover in the following pages, Rodney King is no ordinary leadership coach. His unorthodox view of martial arts as a way to enrich our performance in everyday life, as well as on the mat, has earned him the tag "Anti-Tough Guy" by some of his cage-fighting contemporaries in the field of mixed martial arts (MMA).

His passion for taking in the bigger picture—honoring the wisdom of ancient philosophers such as Marcus Aurelius, and spiritual sages such as the Buddha, Krishnamurti, and Thich Nhat Hanh—and for acknowledging the importance of Warrior ethics and values, Rodney is viewed both as a hero and a villain by different groups.

But, as you will also learn in these pages, developing the "mental game" is not for sissies or wimps. On the contrary, it takes courage, self-discipline, and long hours of often grueling practice to take on the task of training your "Inner Warrior." Having superior martial arts skills helps too, of course.

After decades coaching thousands of others on how to improve their "game," Rodney has developed a six-step system for training and applying the "secrets" of mind-body peak performance to leadership, in fields as diverse as sports, law-enforcement, security, and business. In Rodney's hands, martial arts' training becomes *performance* training, applicable in just about any situation that requires quick-reactions, a clear mind, managed emotions, and a mind-body unity ready and willing to respond to any challenge.

Half Moon Bay, California
January, 2015

Part 1: Getting Tough

Preface

Until my late 20s, I felt like I had been fighting my whole life. Brought up on the south side of Johannesburg, in South African government housing (similar to "the projects" in the USA), I learned early on that what really mattered was not how smart you were, but whether you were tough enough. Growing up, I often felt trapped in a really bad nightmare—and I wanted to wake up.

But tough times build strong character, and I was determined to survive the school bullies and the mean streets of my neighborhood. That's how I discovered martial arts, and set the course for the rest of my life. If I hadn't started training in karate and boxing, I wouldn't be standing today in front of business leaders, entrepreneurs, and other success-minded people . . . coaching them on how to tap into their inner game.

Things turned rough in my teens. My abusive, alcoholic mother kicked me out of the house at 17 and, as a result, I never finished high school. I found myself sleeping on the streets with less than $20 in my pocket—yet today I consult with leaders of industry, train top security forces, and run my own international business. Martial arts taught me to be resilient, to embrace my fears, to develop laser-like focus, and to never give up. Having developed those qualities (I *had* to!), I went back to school, put myself through college, and am currently completing my Ph.D in Embodied Leadership. Over the years, I have taught special-force military operators and law enforcement officers how to develop an unstoppable mind, needed for success on the battlefield, or on city streets, and how to survive when all else fails.

You see, I did wake up from that nightmare. What I learned on the mat as a martial artist, helped me not only take on those tough, mean streets of Johannesburg, but it empowered me to take on *life*, full throttle, and to succeed.

What I learned, and what I teach my clients today, may surprise you. Being tough is not about aggression, violence, or killer instinct. In fact, everything I teach is the complete opposite: it's about having a Buddha mind, and a Warrior body—Zen in the midst of chaos. Most important it works! It worked for me, and it works for my clients not only on the dojo floor, but in their lives and careers.

What follows is the story of the hard-learned lessons that not only taught me to become a successful martial artist, coach, and entrepreneur—but also enabled my clients to successfully take on "the martial arts of everyday life." The techniques that I coach, not only enhance performance in a fight, but also enable my clients to perform at their best in all aspects of life.

My motto has always been: "Performance is performance"—meaning it doesn't matter whether it is in the ring where "performance" shows up as self-defense, or on the street, or in the boardroom during tough negotiations, or, indeed, at home dealing with everyday domestic challenges (I now often find myself negotiating with my thirteen-year-old son).

The ingredients for successful performance—*in all areas of life*—transcend the situation. The "inner tools" that shape success are perennial and universal. That's what I discovered as I struggled to survive on the mean streets, and then developed into a system to help myself and my clients thrive, as we face the inevitable challenges of today's competitive world.

—Rodney King M.A. RSME
Johannesburg, 2014

Introduction

In *Full-Contact Living,* I share six principles that have helped shape my success—not only on the mat as a martial artist, but in life. Over the years I've learned that it's not what we do on the outside that matters most; it's how well we manage who we are on the inside. This insight is central to my approach to martial arts, life and leadership coaching. Baseball legend Yogi Berra quipped: "Ninety percent of the game is half mental." I guess he was saying that being great at anything comes down to how well you win the battles inside your mind. The big question, of course, is how do you actually make that happen? How do you build the inner game for success?

I developed the following life-changing principles over almost three decades of martial arts practice, through coaching thousands of people on the mat, surviving thousands of rounds of sparring, and through several years working as security outside the roughest nightclubs in Johannesburg. No one ever taught me these principles directly. I discovered them the hard way: Repeatedly facing life-threatening situations, and realizing I had to out-perform my adversaries, or suffer the consequences. I quickly learned that my greatest strength was: *Understanding myself.* It didn't happen all at once, though. I cultivated a persistent attitude of wanting to truly understand how my mind and body function together in moments of crisis.

I was determined to discover what happens *on the inside,* trying to figure out how on one day I was able to operate at full-tilt, one-hundred percent, in the zone — yet the very next day I found myself choking? The result of this personal inner research, you now hold in your hands. I believe anyone can apply these principles to achieve sustained peak performance—not only on the mat, but in the rest of life.

I use these principles personally, daily, whenever I find myself out of my comfort zone, for example standing in front of a room of strangers having to present a lecture or give a demonstration. From direct personal experience, I know these principles work, and I have taught them to special force operators, where making a mistake means paying the ultimate price.

The main message about my life that I want to convey in this book is simple enough: *Success in full-contact living is an inside job!* That's it in a nutshell. Yes, I've had great success sparring in dojos around the world (and I don't ever want to diminish the satisfaction that brings); but by far the greatest reward is how well I perform in what I call *the martial arts of everyday life*.

Right up-front, I want to be honest about this: While the six principles I cover in this book do really *work,* they are not the only path to peak performance. However, they do lay a solid foundation for an embodied philosophy, and a special kind of awareness that can lead to a more sustained, and consistent performance—in any of life's challenges that involve mastery of the mind-body connection.

My goal for this book; is to weave practical know-how and personal narrative into a valuable "manual for life," that readers can use to help them improve their "game"—however they define it for themselves. As a side note, my friend and student Andy Robertson, who did all the wonderful artwork for this book, has told me that training on the mat, and embodying the six principles, has made him a better artist.

This book, then, tells the story of my own journey as a martial artist, and summarizes the important life lessons I have learned along the way—lessons that have positively informed and transformed my life inside and outside the dojo. While the following pages offer a self-help guide for martial artists, seeking to enhance their performance on the mat or in the ring, they also offer a helping hand to anyone who struggles with the martial arts of everyday life.

Steps to Success

The six big ideas outlined in this book, will help you achieve optimal success in virtually any performance environment—whether you want to improve your sparring game, climb a rock face, surf a monster wave, sky dive or deep dive, sail over the horizon, defend your neighborhood or country, protect your family . . . in short, to get the most out of your career and life. In fact, you could think of this book as a manual for how to "hack" your life for peak performance.

Although I've organized this book around the six prime principles for achieving peak performance, no single idea works on its own. All six principles are interconnected. You need to understand and apply them all, in order to be truly successful. If you are musically inclined, you could view these principles as notes in a symphony—each individual note is essential, but the power of the music comes from how well the notes work together. In the same way, each principle is essential for success; but how you integrate them in your life, determines how well you will succeed.

I recommend first reading this book cover to cover, and then, once you know and understand the material, feel free to come back and dive in as you need to, from time to time.

To help you get started, and to orient you on your journey, the following outline of the book will serve as your guide—your "map to success."

Back-story: Martial Arts Saved My Life

Literally, adversity built the courage and determination I needed to be successful as a martial artist, entrepreneur, and a dad. This chapter gives you a glimpse into my life growing up, and will set the tone for the rest of the book.

The Language of Embodiment

You will find some really big ideas in this book. I want to present them in a way that not only makes them accessible, but also doesn't "dumb" them down. This chapter explains key terminology used throughout this book. Since some of the ideas might be new to you, reading this quick guide will help you make sense of the core ideas. While I take philosophy seriously, I have tried to make unfamiliar words easy to understand. This is essentially my life story and a manual for peak performance—it is not intended as an academic treatise. In fact, I'm aware that some of the key ideas covered here are still hotly debated. Feel free to alter and adapt them for your own use.

Principle 1: The *Wabi-Sabi* of Peak Performance

Naturally, we want everything to be perfect in life. However, as the French philosopher Voltaire wisely observed: "Perfection is the enemy of the good." Or, as Confucius said: "Better a diamond with a flaw than a pebble without." My version: *"Perfection is the enemy of success."*

You will never achieve your goals as long as you hold out for perfection. I learned an important lesson early on: While you wait for things to be *just right*, life happens around you, and you miss most of it. John Lennon said something similar: "Life is what happens while you are busy making other plans." The sooner you come to grips with this, the sooner you can achieve personal success. In Japanese, this idea is captured in the phrase *"wabi-sabi"*—which, loosely translated, means something like "the perfection of imperfection." In this chapter, we will explore the paradox of imperfection needed for perfect peak performance.

Principle 2: Buddha Mind, Warrior Body

Thinking isn't inherently bad, but what you focus on can be. Reflecting on past mistakes and planning for the future, are crucial for long-term achievement. But when it comes to performance in the moment, where it matters most, past and future can get you into trouble. When your thoughts wander away from the present moment, you can easily get caught up in a mental vortex, spin out of control, and lose touch with the reality of what is *actually happening*. The present moment is the only time you can ever take action. That's why mental clarity in the *present moment* is crucial for taking action that leads to success. However, being fully present and aware can be hard work because so much of what goes on around us in the media, in education, in society in general, snatches our attention away from us, slinging our thoughts into the past or the future. In this chapter, I will show you how to achieve more focus in the midst of life's chaos.

Principle 3: Body Attitude Matters

How you hold your body not only changes your physiology, it also changes how you think and feel. How you show up in the world matters more than you think. Scientists have discovered that some very simple gestures, such as how you shape your mouth, can affect your mental attitude. Bottom line: Although our minds and bodies are different, they always go together. What happens in your body affects what happens in your mind—and vice versa. In this chapter, I will introduce you to *body attitude*, and why it is essential for peak performance in any endeavor.

Principle 4: Surf the Edge of Chaos

This chapter introduces you to the power of *mindfulness in action*—how to "surf the edge of chaos," or, as my kid says, "live like a boss" (meaning "master what you do in life"). Mindfulness is a state of being, where you are able to just *be present* without judging the outcome of your performance. It involves not becoming attached to what you are thinking, or getting hooked to your emotions or bodily sensations. When you can master your mind by being *present as the observer* of your thoughts and feelings, you develop what I call *having a fluid mind*. Mindfulness is crucial when dealing with difficult emotions and thoughts. Sounds like something we all need, right? However, for mindfulness to be truly effective, you have to be able to apply it in action, not just sitting on a cushion in meditation.

Principle 5: Exhale—Take Charge of Your Breath

Breathing isn't just something you do to stay alive. *How you breathe* also affects *how you act*. More and more, medical science reveals how emotions such as fear and aggression are responsible for many modern-day maladies, including anxiety and hypertension. As you will see in this chapter, these emotions kick in when our sympathetic nervous system gets activated. It's called the "fight or flight" response, which is still a key area of medical research. One thing we already know for sure: the sympathetic nervous system is intimately connected to how we breathe. When fear or aggression erupts in our system, we automatically tend to hold our breath, and our breathing becomes shallow and irregular. This is a striking example of the mind-body connection. The good news: It works both ways. By consciously taking charge of how we breathe, we can change how our nervous system works. Some simple techniques can make a big difference whenever negative emotions dominate our state of mind. One of the simplest is to simply *exhale* forcefully and *breathe in* deeply. Believe it or not, learning how to take charge of your breathing can work wonders in all kinds of performance. It's like learning how to speak to your nervous system.

Principle 6: Roll with the Punches

The ability to bounce back from setbacks is the mark of a true peak performer. However, resilience takes work. This chapter teaches you how to cultivate greater resilience, by embracing more challenges in life, and by learning how to "play the game" in ways that can turn adversity into opportunity. Although this is Principle # 6, in some ways, it is the first one I ever learned. As you will see from my life story, I had plenty of adversity to contend with in my youth. But something in me pushed me to rise to the occasion, and despite mistakes and setbacks, to never give up. I learned to "roll with the punches," both literally and metaphorically. Resilience is a keystone of success—however that shows up in your life.

The Meta-Principle: Become an IGAMER

I conclude this book by summarizing and integrating the *Six Principles of Peak Performance* into a "meta" principle—one overarching principle I call "IGAMER." Don't worry what that acronym means—it will all become clear by the end of the book. For now, you just need to know that the secret to "full-contact living" is to cultivate your own IGAMER approach to life. This book shows you how.

Back-story: Martial Arts Saved My Life

To say "I owe my life to martial arts" is no understatement. It saved me from the bullies growing up, it kept me sane during my mother's explosive alcoholic out-bursts, and, for several years, it literally saved my life as a doorman outside some of South Africa's roughest night clubs. It kept me safe in the ring and on the mat when physically challenged—but most importantly, it gave me the confidence to achieve personal and professional success. Exactly how martial arts enabled me to succeed, and the lessons I learned, might not be what you expect.

Before I get into my story, I want to first bring you up to date on my status as a martial arts fighter and coach. While few people outside the world of mixed mar-tial arts (MMA) will even know of my existence, I have achieved a considerable degree of success and notoriety in my own field. I have many good friends and other people who support my unorthodox approach to martial arts (more on that later). But, precisely because I have a different approach, I also have many de-tractors, perhaps even enemies—tough-guys in MMA who think I've "sold out." As it happens, I don't think that to succeed in this sport (or life in general) you need to be violent and aggressive to the point where "winning at all costs" is all that matters. As a result, in some quarters, I am perceived and tagged as the "anti-tough-guy."

But I wasn't always considered the anti-tough-guy of martial arts—in fact, I was that Tough-Guy! And that's where my story begins . . .

Being a tough guy was not a choice—it was a necessity. I thought I needed to be tough to be taken seriously in the world of modern martial arts. On the streets, I had to learn to protect myself in whatever ways worked—being tough was not just an option, it was literally life or death. When I later took up martial arts professionally, I imported that mentality into the sport because I thought I needed to be the Tough-Guy to succeed in that world.

To be honest, I didn't take up martial arts to become the "ultimate fighter," or to be a fearless tough-guy. Throughout my life, I have always been somewhat of a "Reluctant Warrior". For me, it was always more a case of cultivating a "tough guise" rather than being a tough guy. Putting on the tough guise, however, enabled me to survive.

Growing up, I always felt like the odd kid out. Besides feeling awkward in my own body as a child, I felt unaccepted where I lived. My childhood in Johannesburg was surrounded by violence and insecurity. It was a harsh environment to grow up in—especially for a soft-spoken, creative kid, like I was, who hated confrontation. I was bullied severely as a child, not only in my neighborhood, but more so at school. Having my head flushed in the toilet, arriving home with a bloody nose, torn shirt, and drawing pins put on my school chair . . . these were just a few of the torments I had to endure on a daily basis growing up.

Three incidents stand out in my memories of pre-primary school. In Grade two, I was stalked and bullied by a kid named CM, who, on several occasions, cut the back of my legs with a razor blade, and who also beat me up every time the teacher left the classroom. He was not alone by any means: Like him, most of the kids at my school were extreme bullies too.

In third grade, while I was sick in bed with German measles, the trouble-making kids used me as a scapegoat by branding me as their gang leader (I didn't even know what a gang was at that age). I wasn't guilty, but it didn't stop the head mistress from punishing me, and I spent several months at breaks with my nose pressed up against the flag pole in the school yard, while the kids who put me there had a good laugh at my expense. In those days, corporal punishment was still acceptable, and so the headmistress took it upon herself to strike me with her cane more than the maximum of six that was allowed. The punishment seemed so extreme and unfair; that I reacted by pulling the cane from her hands and striking her in the face. Not surprisingly, that almost got me expelled from school. But, I guess, because violence was so endemic—among students and teachers alike—they let me stay on.

I attended several schools growing up, mainly in impoverished neighborhoods, where they cared little about the kids. Teachers mostly looked the other way when the bullies ganged up on unfortunate kids like me—probably because many of the teachers were bullies too. For example, being racked over the knuckles with a wooden ruler for not concentrating in class happened daily.

Given those early experiences, I developed an uncontrollable anxiety and fear just thinking about school—a condition that lasted well in to my 20s. Even today, my heart starts racing, and I feel sick to my stomach, when I go to pick up my own kids from school. I know this is totally unreasonable, as they go to a great school with caring teachers and staff—nothing like the place I had to endure as a kid. Nevertheless, my early experiences were so traumatic, the memory remains imprinted in my body.

Growing up without ever knowing my father, I became an easy target for the bullies. My mother, although she was a quiet woman—reminded me of Dr. Jekyll and Mr. Hyde when she got drunk. She suffered from alcoholism for most of her life, until she was diagnosed with terminal cancer; and then, and only then, was she suddenly able to stop drinking. For the most part, she was not interested in my life, so I pretty much got on with trying to survive and doing my own thing. After years of vainly pleading with her to stop drinking, telling her how it was ruining my life, she finally found the strength and motivation to quit only in the face of her own death. But by then I had almost stopped talking to her.

When I was 17, she kicked me out of the house in a drunken rage, and I found myself sleeping on a park bench (where I used to play as a kid). Destitute and alone, with less than $20 in my pocket, I had to survive the mean streets of Johannesburg. Needless to say, I never finished high school. A few years later, I briefly reunited with my mom on her deathbed. She died on the way to the hospital in the back of my car, held by my wife Louise.

I didn't have many friends growing up. I was an outsider, and although I loved playing sports, I never understood the fierce need to compete. I still feel that way today. In a school where only the best players were chosen to play sports, and kids like me who had no talent for the game, had to watch from the bench, fuelled my disdain for competitive sports even further. Later, when I began to compete in karate and boxing, I learned to fight to win, mostly out of fear of being physically hurt or humiliated. If I didn't win, I was made to feel like a loser. My boxing coach once slapped me in the face because he caught me crying. "Toughen up boy," he said.

Yet, ironically, boxing and martial arts became my escape from my troubled childhood. I went to see as many martial arts movies as I could, and then took up the art itself. I remember, among my earliest and fondest memories of martial arts, watching old Chinese *kung fu* movies on the reel at my uncle's house. Even at age six, I was captivated by how, through rigorous and arduous training, the main character was able to transform himself from a weak unassuming man, into the hero—using *kung fu* to beat the bad guys tormenting his village, and, along the way, getting the girl of his dreams.

After being kicked out of my home, I found a half-way house that took me in. Soon after that, still just 17, I signed up for compulsory military service. I found myself part of the VIP Protection Unit. An uncompromising military section, built on strict discipline. Equipped with my karate and boxing skills, I decided from the first day on the base, that I wasn't going to allow anyone to push me around. This no-nonsense attitude caught the eye of the regimental sergeant major (RSM), who called me into his office: "King, I hear the men are scared of you? We need someone like you. Here you go. You are the new platoon sergeant."

And there I was, with the most hated job in my unit. A big bull's-eye on my back, everyone was out to get me. The army made me tough. So tough, in fact, that I became the hand-to-hand combat instructor for the unit. On some level, I think the RSM regretted giving me that position, but I got the job done, and I wasn't scared to use violence to make it happen. On the final day, as I was leaving and heading back into civilian life, he called me over and muttered: "King, I am glad you're leaving this man's army."

With all these negative experiences growing up, and having to watch my back constantly in the army, I grew bitter, angry, and violent. I was all about the fight. Winning was all that mattered. I had developed a serious reputation as someone you didn't want to mess with.

But I didn't like what I had become. A decade ago, in a moment of insight, I remembered what drew me to martial arts in the first place. It was not so much the effectiveness of skills, or being good at fighting, but rather its transformative potential.

I decided to overhaul my entire martial arts approach. I had to find a positive expression for my fighting skills, something that would positively change lives for the better. Otherwise, I was going to quit. For two long years I suffered from serious depression, but told no one. After all, I had a reputation, guys were scared of me, and I was at the top of my physical game. I was the Alpha.

When I finally had the courage to tell everyone that I had decided to go down a different path, they all stared back at me. *Sport Illustrated South Africa* referred to me as the "father of mixed martial arts in South Africa." And I was. At a pivotal meeting at my gym, aptly named Street Tough, all the people sitting in front of me I had personally groomed to be fighters. These guys were tough, uncompromising; hard. But when I told them about my new direction, they looked back at me, uncomprehending, as if waiting for the punch line that would reveal the "joke." But I wasn't joking. I was deadly serious. Looking at their faces, I could see they thought I had lost the plot. I told them I wanted to return to the original reason I had taken up martial arts: I loved and valued it as a path to personal transformation. I couldn't do it the "tough" way anymore. I didn't want anything to do with it if it was all about violence, winning, and beating up other people—even as sport. If I was going to spend my time in the ring or on the mat, it had to be positive, add value, and change lives for the better. However, given the state of the game, I couldn't see that happening—not without a new vision and leadership.

Ninety percent of those at that meeting left my studio within two months and never came back. Even though, deep down, I knew I had made the right decision,

I felt as I did as a small child—shunned, isolated, and alone. I wanted to quit, give it all up and head off to Thailand to teach English.

But, by then, resilience had taken root in my soul, and I didn't quit. In fact, the changes I made sky-rocketed my success—in martial arts, in business, and in my personal life. Today, one of the things that get me most excited is when I see how my approach to martial arts does the same for my clients.

I went back to school, received a master's degree in leading innovation and change, and at the time of writing this I am completing my doctoral degree at the University of Leicester's School of Management. I started two programs, focused on life performance coaching using martial arts. And my "unorthodox" Crazy Monkey Defense method is now taught in more than fifteen countries around the world.

Not bad for a boy who started out with only $20 in his pocket.

This, of course, is the short version of my story, but it captures the essence of what I want this book to communicate. With this background, the rest of the book will focus on the lessons I have learned along the way—the Six Principles of Embodied Peak Performance. This is what I teach today, and I work hard to live by these values and insights every day.

This book then, is about *the martial arts of everyday life*—how to prepare for it, head on, through full-contact living.

The Language of Embodiment

Throughout this book, I have tried to make the main storyline accessible, and also to make some big ideas easy to understand. I really mean "big ideas," many of which still surround themselves in raging debates in philosophy, psychology, and academia at large. I'm aware that the way I have presented some of these ideas would likely make many academics cringe because; I have deliberately avoided complex analysis in favor of simple, straightforward discussions.

My number one goal is to a write a user-friendly book, which anyone, without previous background in philosophy and psychology could instantly use. I didn't want to engage in any obscure debates on major theories in the field of embodiment, or to critique specific theories. I leave that for the academics (although I realize they react to over-simplification).

Again: To emphasize this point: I did not set out to write a *philosophical* treatise. No, this is a *pragmatic* book, about how to dive head-first into life; and although I do draw on some new and ancient ideas, and principles from philosophy and psychology; everything in these pages is rooted firmly in my own personal experience—in life and on the mat. I show how I have successfully used these principles to become a super-successful martial artist, and entrepreneur, equally committed to inspiring my clients to achieve the same level of success in their lives.

When I first began teaching these concepts and principles, I did so simply through the success I had with my own life-experiments. Trying to express these pre-verbal insights and ideas in words, then, can be difficult. I struggled with that for many years, searching for the "right" words, and more times than not, I would simply say to anyone who wanted to know what I had learned: "Let's get on the mat and I'll show you." As it turns out, many of the ideas I have been intuitively coaching for the past decade (and presented in this book), are now backed by research, and where possible, I have tried to point to those findings.

But beyond the research, and my story, from time to time I will use terminology that might be unfamiliar. Don't let that put you off. In every case, the *words* are only pointers, and what really matters is the experience behind them—my experience and yours too. In this chapter, I will introduce you to some of the key terms that will help you understand the main points covered in these pages. However, even though I have taken care to explain these foundational ideas, I cannot emphasize strongly enough that what matters most, is not the language, but how you *use and apply* the key ideas. Bottom line: Use my words as guides, as pointers to direct you in your own actions. *Find out for yourself what works and what doesn't as Bruce Lee would say.* You might even come up with your own terminology that fits better for you. That is all that really matters to me in the end.

So, go for it …. Let's start with one of the key phrases you will come across time and again in this book, or in my workshops: ***Embodied-Mind Performance*** (EMP). Part of me would love that as the title for this book, but it's just not as captivating. I created the term EMP years ago when I was asked to coach special force military operators on how to manage how their minds affect their body's performance on the battlefield. My job was to give them tools for achieving sustained success in combat. For that series of embodied lectures, I had to come up with a name, and EMP seemed the best way to describe what I was asking them to achieve in training. Using my martial arts background, I combined physical martial application, along with drills, and embodied practices (the *art*) in "martial arts" to teach these operators a real, action-learning experience. I didn't want to ask them to sit in a lecture hall, watching and listening to a PowerPoint presentation.

The outcome was very successful.

During that training series, I referred to the performance process as engaging the "embodied-mind," where I made the case that; true inner performance facilitates outer success. It is not just what one does in one's head (i.e. thinking) that enhances performance—on the contrary, effective performance begins by *thinking with the entire body* as an integrated whole. Here, mind and body are not separate, but one.

While the phrase, "embodied-mind performance," might seem a bit of a mouthful, it actually means something quite specific and straightforward. But before I break it down into its three components—"embodied," "mind," and "performance," I first want to make a crucial distinction.

The point I want to make, involves the difference between what I will call the "outer body" and the "inner body" (or "embodied body"). The outer body should be no mystery: It is what we see with our senses—typically sight and touch. It is what you see in the mirror, and what other people see about you. The "inner body," on the other hand, refers to *what it feels like to be you from the inside,* inhabiting the world—how you experience your muscle tension, your balance, breath, heartbeat, and so on—what some psychologists, and somatic specialists, call "proprioception." In fact, you could think of your inner body as your "kinesthetic body"—in other words, your inner, subjective experience of yourself.

Your lived experience of your own body performs three roles in life: First, the body is *socially constructed* —meaning that we think and talk about our bodies, based on what we have learned from society. Second, the body is a *social relational representation of power*—meaning how we perceive and use our bodies, is determined to a great extent by the power relations among people. (A typical example, of course, is that men are conditioned to believe they are stronger than women. While this is true to some extent, in terms of pure muscle strength, it has nothing to do with skill or superiority.) And third, the *lived body*—meaning our experience of *being in the world* as an embodied, feeling, conscious person.

From this perspective, then, embodiment (i.e. *you*) itself is *inter—corporeal*. This unfamiliar term means, simply, that despite what we have been conditioned to think, our bodies do not exist as standalone blocks of skin, muscle, blood, and bone. On the contrary, our bodies exist in constant dialogue with other bodies in our environment (human and non-human), and these relationships "construct" how we think and feel about our own "individual" body. The paradox here, in case you missed it, is this: We believe we are independent and individual bodies, *because that's what we have learned from our interactions with other bodies around us!* Our sense of individuality emerges from the undeniable fact: That we are always interacting in a network of other embodied beings. That's what "inter-corporeal" means.

The experience of being embodied, then, is never a private affair—even though most of us think that it is. Rather it is always, and already mediated by, our continual interactions with other human and non-human bodies. Both Foucault and Bourdieu, (two prominent twentieth-century French philosophers), saw the subjective body as informed, or "constructed," by social and historical factors.

Therefore, there is no gap between mind, body, and a person's experience of the world. Your experience of things, then, arises out of your embodiment in the world. Once stated, this should seem so obvious—yet like many obvious things right under our noses, it is easily missed. The experience of being *you,* arises from, and connects *you,* with the world around you. In other words, we are all formed equally by the world, by culture, and the society we live in.

As you read this book, then, try to be aware that some of the things you tend to do automatically as habit, and may want to change, most likely arose from your social and historical conditioning. We all carry our social and historical heritage in just about everything we do. As many psychologists have shown: We never see the world *as it is,* but only as we have been *trained to view it.*

With this little detour into embodied philosophy, we can now focus on unpacking the key term I introduced earlier—*embodied-mind performance.* Let's take the last item first:

Performance. We are all familiar with the idea of performance. It refers to how we act and express ourselves to achieve a certain outcome. In many areas of life—including the arts, sports, business, education and health—performance often follows practice.

First, we practice the ideas presented in this book to learn how to apply them—and then we do certain pre-designed exercises to train our bodies and minds to act or perform effectively in certain ways appropriate to the task (also covered in this book). Next, after we feel we have achieved a targeted level of accomplishment, we go public and take what we have learned into a performance environment (on the mat against an opponent, during a meeting at work, etc.).

"Going public," though, doesn't necessarily always mean performing in front of a large audience. It may simply refer to using what you have learned in this book in your day-to-day, mundane life (more about that later).

Performance, then, means *putting into action what you have learned*. With enough practice, taking consistent small steps leads, ultimately, to peak performance. Peak performance, at least as I define it, happens when applied action culminates in a moment (or even an extended period) of pure presence. Peak performance occurs when victory and defeat are no longer relevant, or even internally validated. When one allows the body's natural intelligence to make the right choices, without interference from the judgmental mind. Psychologist Mihaly Csikszentmihalyi, has famously identified this as the state of "flow."

The main intent of this book, then, is to present tools that make peak performance more accessible. By applying the tools presented here, you can achieve peak performance in the heat of the battle (both literally and figuratively), where it matters most—whether sparring with someone, tackling an adversary as a military or law-enforcement specialist, or, less dangerously, in the midst of a presentation at work. Performing at your best—right here, right now—is what this book is ultimately about.

Embodied. Action, of course, always involves our bodies. We are physical beings, living in a physical universe. Nothing ever happens without some physical body moving through space, (whether it's atoms, molecules, cells, arms, fists, legs, or a whole human body). One inescapable fact of life, is, that we are always embodied. As long as we exist in the physical universe, we will have a body.

However, for a very long time the body was neglected, both as an instrument for lived experience, and as one's active embodiment in the world. This goes back as far as Plato's *Phaedo* (about 400 BCE). The Greek philosopher saw the body as negatively interfering with the search for true knowledge. He said that the body interrupted our attention, with all kinds of passions and fancies. In other words, the body distorts reality through its flawed perception, obscured by its appetites and desires. The body, then, was seen as merely a tool in the service of the intellect. This way of thinking of the body (both inner and outer) has dominated Western thinking for centuries, for example, through the spread of Christian theology, which later shaped a lot of early modern philosophy in the West. Philosophies such as idealism, which claim that the only reality is ultimately mind, consciousness, or spirit; downplay the significance, and even the existence, of the body. Due to the influence of Plato and the Church, for centuries, even millennia, the body has been either ignored or dismissed as something evil to be shunned. Even today, modern education focuses on, and celebrates, the mind at the expense of the body. By contrast, in this book, I want to emphasize and celebrate the power of effective mind-body integration.

In modern times (meaning since the dawn of the scientific revolution in the seventeenth century), the split between mind and body goes back to the French philosopher René Descartes (sorry René, I do hammer you a quite a bit in this book). Descartes' philosophy of separating the thoughts of the mind, from the actions of the body (dualism), greatly influenced Western philosophy, resulting in the dominant idea that our mind is separate from, and acts independently of, our body. In an attempt to restore balance, and overcome the Church's obsession with souls, modern science shifted attention back onto the physical world.

Viewing mind and body as two different kinds of reality, has penetrated not only the worlds of philosophy and science, but it has also had a profound effect on how ordinary people view the world.

Science has focused exclusively on learning about the physical world, and has ignored the non-physical domain of mind and consciousness. As a result, people tend to see the tangible, physical side of their lives—what they can measure and quantify—as real and important. And that's why people tend to place greater value on their material possessions.

Did you notice the historical paradox in all of this? First, going back to Plato more than two-thousand years ago, and then followed by Descartes about four hundred years ago, Western philosophers split the mind and body apart. Next step, the Church favored the mind half of the equation and regarded the body as a source of sin—something evil to be avoided or transcended. Then, about four-hundred years ago, the scientific revolution began and flipped the mind-body split by focusing on the "body" part—meaning the *physical* world. Mind was shunted aside, and thought of as unimportant.

And here's the paradox: Even though science focuses on matter, it has completely lost sight of *embodiment.* In other words, while science claims to study the world of matter (physics and chemistry) and bodies (biology and neuroscience), it treats matter and bodies as "dead" stuff, with no internal meaning, purpose, or value—without the slightest trace of sentience or intelligence. The "bodies" that science studies are nothing like the bodies you and I inhabit—bodies that tingle with feelings, sensations, emotions, and intelligence. The upshot of the scientific obsession with matter means that the significance of *embodiment* has been ignored or denied.

By now, I hope, you have realized that "embodied" means much more than having an objective physical body (the one you can see in the mirror). It means, instead, a body that *feels itself from inside,* a body that is always alive with intelligence and sentience, never separated from its mind (this is the "internal body" I mentioned earlier). In a word, then, "embodiment" means a *body that tingles with feelings, sensations, intelligence—a body with a mind of its own.* In short: The body that you know from the inside.

By now, of course, it will be clear to you that the position I take in this book departs radically from Plato's and Descartes' mind-body split, from the idealist/religious preoccupation with mind alone, and from the scientific materialist's obsession with matter alone. Unlike Plato, I do not view the body as something that interferes with the search for true knowledge of oneself in the world; nor do I accept Descartes' notion of separate mind and body. Instead, I view mind and body as one—as *mind-body* (or *body-mind)*, forming a holistic, inseparable, unity. *That's* embodiment. I view the body as an active, organic agent that both informs and structures our actions in the world.

This position implies that our behavior arises from actively engaging in the world. Embodiment, therefore, involves the integration of perceptions, thoughts, feelings, and desires expressed through our active engagement and agency in that world. In other words: The body has its own natural intelligence.

Given this perspective, then, a crucial goal of this book is to provide you with the tools that will allow your body's natural intelligence to emerge in the midst of the hustle and bustle of daily living—whether in the dojo on the mat, or elsewhere in your life. Embodiment, therefore, is the key to achieving peak performance—in all aspects of life.

Mind. I've already talked a little bit about mind in relation to the body. Now it's time to say something more specifically about this controversial aspect of reality. Mind is one of those words that get people confused or excited—depending on their level of self-reflection and education. As far as I can tell, philosophers and scientists get both excited and confused when trying to understand and discuss this "ghostly" topic. Ordinary, everyday people tend to shy away from thinking, or talking, about this intangible entity that lives inside our heads and throughout the rest of our body.

Part of the difficulty in talking about mind goes back to, you guessed it: Descartes. He defined mind as having no extension in space, in opposition to bodies that are extended and do take up space. According to Descartes, minds exist as thinking things, so, the nature of mind is to think (and by "thinking" he meant any mental activity, including feelings, or emotions, or making choices). Mind, then, is the capacity to be aware, to think or reflect, to feel, and to choose.

So far so good . . . except for one crucial thing: Our ability to think, reflect, feel, and choose is *always* embodied. Take away or destroy a person's body, and you immediately take away or destroy their mind too. You can't have one without the other.

In philosophy and science, the debate rages on: Does the brain give rise to mind, or does mind give rise to the brain? Putting aside the "experts" for now, have you ever thought about how your mind makes your body move? You have a thought about picking up a glass of water, and then you choose to do so . . . almost instantly your arm reaches out and grabs the glass. *How did that happen?* Your thought and your choice took place in your mind, yet *somehow* those mind-events made part of your body move. *How?* How do mind and body interact?

That is one of the deepest problems in philosophy, and has stirred up raging debates through the centuries.

As we have seen, part of the problem is that when Descartes gave us his definitions of mind and body, he also split them apart. Yes, he's the dude responsible for the infamous "mind-body split," and people have been trying to heal that split ever since. Without going any deeper into the history of philosophy, let's just say that despite his other valuable insights about the nature of mind and body, Descartes' greatest error was to split them apart. It doesn't take a genius to realize that minds and bodies always go together. I bet you've never met a disembodied, free-floating mind (how could you?). And everybody you meet has some capacity to be aware of his or her surroundings, and to make choices about what to do next.

In other words: Every body comes with its own mind built in—that's to say, every body has its own natural intelligence, ready to be expressed. And every mind, likewise, is always embodied. In other words, every mind comes with its own body attached. Every mind is grounded in a body. And that's what I mean by "embodied-mind." Think of mind, then, as *you* in your entirety. Body-mind, as one. No separation.

For ease of use, then, when I use the term "embodied-mind" in this book, I am really describing all of you, and when I refer to the thinking mind, I mean what's going on in your head (thoughts, images, etc). However, it's important to keep in mind that while I make a *distinction* between mind and body, for ease of understanding, there never is any real *separation* between them. The distinction is just a useful way for us to think, and talk, about the two decisive components of embodiment. Mind-body, thinking or otherwise, always go together. To wrap this up: "Mind" simply means *being aware*, and "embodied-mind," means that mind and body are one. Your mind is the source of your awareness of where you are located, and the source of all the choices you make to move or redirect yourself from one place to another. Mind, then, means using your mind-body's own natural intelligence so you can make conscious choices, to create embodied change that will lead to peak performance and success.

Somatic Self-Awareness. I've already mentioned a few paradoxes. Here's another one: In this book, I lay out practices and exercises to help you develop somatic awareness of your inner world, so that you can ultimately let go of it ("*soma*" is Latin for "body"). In other words, somatic self-awareness is the intentional "self-awareness" of both your inner and outer body (both how you view your outer/inner body, and how the outer world affects it).

A heightened sense of somatic self-awareness need not disrupt your engagement with the outside world; rather somatic awareness informs all your actions and perceptions. Somatic awareness, your mind-body, connects you with the world itself. If you want your actions to be effective, then they need to respond to, or initiate, changes in your environment, in your reality. That means, then, the best way to work with the reality confronting you is to engage your full mind-body in the moment.

In order to have a "self," we must be able to reflect upon our identities, our actions, and our relationships with others. As such, giving primacy to our embodied-mind, and recognizing how we show up in the world through using it, gives us greater clarity of mind and body, and this, in turn, helps bring greater clarity to the world.

If you want to connect with the world in a meaningful way, then embodiment is the key. Taking a cue from sports performance, as Benita Johnson, Australian long-distance runner has previously noted: Believing in one's ability (an internal state) is a deciding factor among athletes of similar physical strength, training, and shape. An individual's core beliefs are embodied—that is, the beliefs and values that motivate people most consistently are literally felt as sensations in the body (as a *proprioceptive* state). Thus, having the physical skill to be a great athlete does not, on its own, account for winning against other equally skilled athletes. Beyond the physical capabilities of the athlete (which can be measured and quantified), something more intangible—some deeper quality of being—is the decisive factor, leading to an embodied state that enables one person to perform better than another. This insight illuminates the heart of this book: What you do on the inside, the level of skill you have in inner management, will accurately predict how well you do in any endeavor you take on in life.

Through your own personal experience, you know you can acquire bad habits as easily as good ones. The question, then, is how do you rectify the bad habits? One way, advocated in this book, is to adopt a purposeful approach to reflective somatic self-awareness—being in the "flow" in the present moment. Being in the present takes you away from thinking and analyzing, allowing you to focus your perception on the actual reality in front of you. You might wonder what benefit you might get from a practice that takes you beyond thinking—after all, isn't that what all education is about? Training us how to use our intellect to analyze situations, to weigh up the pros and cons before we take action? Yes, indeed, that is what we are educated to believe and to do. And it has its uses.

Clearly, it makes sense to know how to think critically in critical situations. However, many times in life, our thinking mind actually *gets in the way* of effective action. That's because when we get lost in our thoughts, we disconnect ourselves from the present moment. We spend time thinking (or worrying) about what might happen in the future (maybe even just a few moments in the future), or about what happened in the past (perhaps what *just* happened).

But, when our thoughts hook us into the past or the future, they disconnect us from the reality of the present moment. And, in fast-paced circumstances, that can be a real danger—perhaps even the difference between life and death. *Thinking takes time.* And when you don't have time to think, you have to learn to rely on some other aspect of your innate intelligence to guide you—your body's own in-built intelligence, your somatic awareness, your embodied, unified, mind-body.

There's a time for self-reflective thinking, and there's a time for action. The wisdom of 'embodied' peak performance is, *knowing,* when to do what. Great athletes, martial artists, dancers, and other performers *know* when to let go of their thinking minds, and to trust in their body's natural wisdom to guide their actions. That's the secret of peak performance. However, as the term suggests, a "peak" performance takes place in a short burst of time. It is not something to be sustained forever (otherwise, it wouldn't be a *peak* performance). Using your embodied-mind, you let loose at the right moment, and take the right actions to achieve your goal. Once the critical moment has passed, you can relax (but remain alert), and then you have achieved your goal, you can sit back and use your thinking mind to reflect on what you have accomplished (what worked, and what didn't, what could be improved, etc.).

The high art of embodied-mind performance is learning to *feel* when it is time to shift into top gear, and when it is time to relax and reflect. That way, you conserve your energy, ready to burst into action whenever the next critical moment arises. You don't want to try to live life always at your "peak." That would quickly drain your reserves. Better to learn to hop from peak to peak, knowing when to drop down into the troughs or valleys for some well-deserved R&R.

Peak performance, then, involves both interior qualities and exterior behaviors. The interior aspect (your state of mind) is primary and decisive. The observable exterior aspect (how your interior world is outwardly expressed) is secondary. A common cliché says that, "form follows function." However, when we view what's required for peak performance, we could flip that to "function follows form"—meaning your state of mind (your mental "form") determines the quality of your action (your function or performance).

Put another way: The quality of being, experienced and embodied in a person's life, is the major determinant of effectiveness of that person's actions. That is, the art or aesthetic of living—through embodied skills—is the hallmark of highly effective and inspirational people.

Throughout this book, I advocate a process that allows you to engage in corrective, somatic self-awareness. This is achieved through embodied reflection and exercises. The tools presented here allow you to witness your embodied-mind (*you* in your entirety) and what it is doing, while it does it. By witnessing the inner flow of your mind-body and its reactions to the outer world, you gain insight and mindful awareness of your inner world. Using the tools offered in this book, you can create opportunities to engage in corrective, somatic self-awareness, that will make all the difference between average action, and the kind of peak performance required for full-contact living.

Embodied-Mind Performance. And so we've come full circle.

Understanding peak performance, then, involves experiential knowledge that mind and body are not separate. Your success in a high- performance environment does not come from what you do in your head (your thinking mind). It comes from the art of knowing when to *let go* and let your body's natural intelligence take over.

Candace Pert, a neuroscientist and pharmacologist, who discovered the opiate receptor in the brain (the cellular binding site for endorphins), notes that people's immune systems have both a capacity for memory, and a capacity to learn, much as the central nervous system does. The implication is that intelligence is located not only in the brain, but is distributed throughout the body.

Embodied-mind performance, then, means being present in such a way; that you are acutely aware of the state of your inner world. Armed with this awareness (somatic self-awareness), you are now well prepared to put into action (performance) everything you have learned from the exercises and principles offered in this book—all aimed at the goal of achieving excellence-in-action either on the mat, in life, or in your career.

Sculptor and artist Auguste Rodin, who created the famous statue *The Thinker*, wrote in his autobiography *Personal Reminiscence*: ". . . what makes my Thinker think, is that he thinks not only with his brain, with his knitted brow, his distended nostrils, and compressed lips, but with every muscle of his arms, back and legs, with his clenched fist and gripping toes." Rodin recognized that a sculpture had to be made from the inside out; and, in the same light, true personal success needs to be understood from the inside out, so that you can bring your best *self* to the world.

Let's get started . . .

Part 2: Six Principles for Peak Performance

Principle 1

The *Wabi-Sabi* of Peak Performance

"Imperfection clings to a person, and if they wait till they are brushed off entirely, they would spin for ever on their axis, advancing nowhere."

—*Thomas Carlyle*

"Perfection is the enemy of success." Simply put: If we always strive for perfection before committing to action, that's a sure-fire guarantee we will never achieve anything worthwhile. Don't get me wrong: I'm not against perfection (in fact that's a major theme of this book and my life's work). No, I want to draw attention to the fact that *waiting* for the perfect moment, or *striving* for perfection, can keep us stuck where we are—in the mud of life. In other words, the ideal of perfection should never be an excuse for inaction. Rather than waiting for everything to be perfect, it's much better to *prepare* as best you can, then *begin* by taking the first step, and be *aware* of any errors, or missteps, along the way. Use your action and interaction with the world around you as a source of *feedback,* and then *correct* your course as you go. Aim for constant *improvement,* rather than reach for the impossible ideal of pure perfection.

Learn to Love the Mess

If you are ever going to have any success as a martial artist, or in life, you have to begin by accepting that peak performance—success itself—is a process of imperfection. Perfection is an illusion. In martial arts training, for example, we try to get as close to perfection as possible, but in actual application—when faced with a real, uncooperative, resisting opponent—we seek only a satisfactory "approximation" of that perfection. In other words, while perfection is something to consistently aim for, it will likely never be achieved, at least, not how we imagine it to be. Like it or not, we simply do not have that degree of control over anything in life.

My journey into embracing "the mess" (imperfection) began when I read this quote by philosopher Alan Watts: "To Taoism, that which is absolutely still or absolutely perfect is absolutely dead, for without the possibility of growth and change there can be no Tao [the way]. In reality there is nothing in the universe which is completely perfect or completely still; it is only in the minds of men that such concepts exist."

I can't tell you how long it took me to fully understand this. I am not even sure I like the uneasy truth. But, anyone who has sparred with great skill knows that however well you might do in training, it can all quickly fall by the wayside, the moment you face a real opponent. In a real fight, with all its unpredictability and chaos, often the best laid plans of fighters instantly evaporate.

Knowing this, what can we do about it?

Rather than try to overcome imperfection, one should learn to embrace it, to see its beauty. The Japanese have a wonderful term for this: "*wabi-sabi*"—an ability to perceive beauty in imperfection. The character Katsumoto in the *The Last Samurai* captures this understanding. Early in the movie he says, "The perfect blossom is a rare thing. You could spend your life looking for one." But toward the end of the movie, as he gazes upon thousands of cherry blossoms, with his dying breath he says, "Perfect . . . they are all . . . perfect." He has come to understand that perfection is an illusion, and that there is great beauty and possibility in imperfection.

In life, we are constantly pushed and told to be perfect. Mistakes are often ridiculed, or worse, punished. Everyone who has suffered through Western schooling will recognize the intense and relentless focus on getting things "just right," and that making mistakes is frowned upon. As author, and motivational consultant, Marcus Buckingham notes, when a child comes home with a report card, parents typically focus more on any D's or F's than on any B's or A's. As a child, you are instantly sent for extra lessons in those subjects you are failing at. Instead, Buckingham advises parents to focus on their child's strengths: "You grow the most in the area where you already show some natural advantage, some natural area of talent or strength or passion. That's where you start." And the research agrees. According to a survey of more than two million people, Gallup researchers discovered that while weakness-fixing can prevent failure, it is strength-building that actually leads to success in the short and long-term.[1]

The paradox however is that in order to find those strengths, you have to be willing, and be allowed, to make mistakes, to embrace imperfection; and through that experience you can discover what you are really good at (something we will discuss further, later in this book). So, while we strive for perfection in the future, we embrace imperfection in the present, using it as building blocks for growth and development. Research confirms, again and again, that superstars in any field did not start out with overwhelming talent. Sure, they might have started with a slight edge, but the real difference in the long-run, is that they simply worked much, much harder than the rest of us. They have embraced their imperfection and their slight edge, and built on that. What's more, this principle of *building on imperfection* applies in all areas of our lives, including our hobbies and professions.

Martial arts mirrors life in many ways. In traditional martial arts, getting things absolutely right is expected—no deviation from the *sensei's* (teacher's) instructions is allowed. Heaven forbid you ever question why. I first realized something was wrong with unquestioning acceptance of everything the *sensei* taught, when I eventually left the stale, repetitive, cycle of pre-arranged techniques, and found

---

[1] Buckingham, M. & Clifton, D. O. (2001). *Now, discover your strengths.* New York: The Free Press.

myself doing *kumite* (free sparring). Suddenly, everything I had learned went out the window. It simply didn't work.

During my karate days, sitting on the sidelines watching other people spar, I was struck by how little of what we had trained to do in class—especially *kata* (pre-arranged forms)—was transferable to an actual sparring match. Sounds a lot like schooling right? Today, just like those years of *kata* training, I use almost nothing I learned at school. Naturally, given my experience of "bending the rules" in martial arts, I wonder if schools teach our children what they most need to know?

And so, one of my earliest realizations: Not only is perfection an illusion; trying to be perfect actually leads to stagnation (as Alan Watts noted earlier). While we may not live in a perfect world, we do live in a world filled with possibilities. But, moving from possibilities to real accomplishments requires action—not action *tomorrow* when you think everything will be perfect, but rather action *right now*, especially when you know everything isn't perfect. As bestselling author, and personal development trainer, Marie Forleo noted, so many budding entrepreneurs fail because they never get started. They are constantly waiting for everything to be just perfect. Perfection is the enemy of action.

I can't tell you how many times prospective clients have come to my gym, watched a class, and then afterwards, when asked what they thought and if they would like to join, replied: "I loved it . . . but I want to get fit first, then I'll come back." Guess what? They never do. For this reason, I don't allow anyone to ever just watch a class I coach. You have to get in and do it, and not wait for everything to be perfect with your fitness, or whatever "excuse" you hint on to avoid getting started.

I learned the hard way: I will never be one-hundred percent ready for anything. This is true for all of us, including you: You have to take some risk, launch yourself into action, and then figure out the rest as you go. Marc Ecko, American fashion designer, entrepreneur, and artist, in a video interview with Chase Jarvis, said much the same when he talked about taking action: telling his team that all they need to do is "…just get in the vicinity . . . like 70 percent," and then, "because I know I am smart enough, or we are self-aware enough, that we will make up that delta between the 70 and the 100 percent."

I realize how scary this can be for many people. But it's not their fault. They have been conditioned to believe that everything has to be "just right" before they can move to the next level. Schooling did this, your parents probably did this too—and, as adults, you belong to a society designed to ensure you continue to conform. Every single piece of advertising and marketing repeatedly tells us how imperfection is bad, perfection is good. Just think of the photo-shopped models on the covers of magazines; we all know no one really looks so perfect in real life. Marketing is designed to make us all feel inadequate with who we are, and where we are right now.

My wife teaches learning through creative movement. She often comments on how kids under five need little or no encouragement to explore something new. Even though they don't know how to do it, they are happy to throw themselves into the endeavor. They haven't yet been tainted by the "perfection virus." But, she says, once past six, kids lose this innate freedom to explore their full potential, without first knowing where it will take them. From that age on, they care more about what other people will think, or how other people have told them things should be—rather than exploring being themselves.

Ironically, martial arts—especially traditional forms—initially killed this innate desire in me to explore, regardless of the outcome. Only when I took up boxing did things begin to change. Karate taught me predictability: Boxing taught me how to surf the edge of chaos (more about this in later chapters).

Boxing is unpredictable. You don't know if your opponent is going to jab, cross or throw a hook, until it is right on top of you. When I was learning *karate kata,* it seemed almost soothing (except when we had to spar), whereas boxing really frustrated me. This puzzled me. Only much later in life, after I began to study about how the human brain works, did I realize why: Our brains love coherence, structure, and order. This is why so much of our schooling and organizations demand to have everything orderly and structured (at least they try really hard to achieve this). It's also one of the best ways to keep us in line and under control. But, as most of us know from experience, schooling ill prepares us for the challenges of adult life. Like boxing, life, too, is also chaotic and unpredictable—while you are making plans, life happens—in others words, life is imperfect . . . *wabi-sabi.*

One of the hardest lessons I had to learn in my martial arts journey is this: Seeking perfection, or even predictability, is to seek an illusion. While the human brain has evolved to seek structure and order, sparring with an unpredictable opponent quickly teaches us that we also need to train our minds (and brains) to respond spontaneously to unpredictable events, and that this ability is also necessary for effective performance . . . both on the mat, and in life in general. When facing a real-life opponent, intent on beating you, all careful planning quickly goes out the window.

Krishnamurti, a spiritual teacher, observed: "One is never afraid of the unknown; one is afraid of the known coming to an end." Ah, how true! In martial arts practice, students often want all the answers about how to deal with an opponent. They think they need to know what to do next, as if having an idea (or, worse, some theory,) will be the magic elixir they're seeking. Unfortunately, life (or martial arts) doesn't work that way. Students trip themselves up when they become fixated on attaining knowledge, in the sense of accumulating more and more technique. I've been around long enough to "read their minds." They think: "If I just learn one more technique, all my frustrations will go away"—as if building a repertoire of techniques will one day turn into a "magic shield" that will protect them from any attack. Yet, as both my own experience, and the science of psychology show, the more we rely on thinking (a cognitive function), the less we tune into our bodies closing down the powerful action of embodied intelligence or "flow" as psychologist Mihaly Csikszentmihalyi calls it. The more we try to hold onto pre-planning and prediction, especially in challenging action situations, the less we are able to act effectively.

In general, as Krishnamurti noted, people are afraid of the known coming to an end; and so they search for more knowledge, and hold onto what they already "know," all in the vain hope of finding answers—even when the "answers" are no longer valid for the situation they now find themselves in. It reminds me of the famous quote attributed to Einstein, to the effect that "insanity is doing the same thing over and over again and expecting different results."

Ironically, the true application of knowledge, in martial arts or life, requires translating, or transforming, knowledge from the thinking mind into embodied action. And here's the clincher: In order to translate knowledge into action, we have to move into the unknown. In other words, there's really no way to hold onto tangible knowledge once you decide to express it through the body in action.

As the late Richard Feynman, a world-renowned physicist, so eloquently put it: "I can live with doubt and uncertainty and not knowing. I think it is much more interesting to live not knowing than to have answers that might be wrong. If we will only allow that, as we progress, we remain unsure, we will leave opportunities for alternatives. We will not become enthusiastic for the fact, the knowledge, the absolute truth of the day, but remain always uncertain. . . . In order to make progress, one must leave the door to the unknown ajar."

A good starting point is to accept, that just because something might seem imperfect doesn't make it unworkable. Applying knowledge, therefore, requires action, and action, by its very nature, always takes place in the present moment, where neither answers (past) nor questions (future) exist. The present moment is also precisely where *wabi-sabi* resides. The beauty of imperfection, then, calls on us to fully embrace the moment—and, as anyone who has tried to "live in the moment" realizes, it takes a lot of practice. I'm not just talking about practices such as meditation, I'm referring to acting in the moment in all kinds of embodied activities—life, work, and, of course, martial arts. Much of this book is dedicated to the pursuit of this ideal.

Danger and Opportunity

The Chinese have a wonderful term, *wei-ji*, composed of two characters that represent both "danger" and "opportunity." One of the greatest lessons that I ever learned on the mat is this: Whatever you happen to be thinking, or feeling, does not determine the outcome. For example, many times when I have felt least like training, making up all kinds of excuses not to go to the gym, yet "forced" myself to go nevertheless, I ended up having an amazing experience. Despite the fact that I just didn't feel in the "perfect" mood, or the "perfect" head-space, to get on the mat, somehow (mainly through feeling guilty), I got myself there. Often on such days, regardless of how I was feeling beforehand, everything somehow came together. Conversely, on days I felt amped to workout, knowing exactly what I was going to do, and couldn't wait to get there, I had the most awful training experience. Things just went wrong.

This has happened to me so often that I have come to realize, that how we feel or think has little to do with how we perform—as long as we make a choice to act. Once in motion, the body has its own wisdom, its own agenda (formed over millions of years of evolution), and it knows what to do, if it is just trusted to do so. Most of the time, our job is to simply get our thinking and judging minds out of the way. Perfection embraces imperfection—that's really what *wabi-sabi* means. Another way to say the same thing: "Perfection is simply accepting what is."

The two kinds of experiences I just described—not wanting to train and really wanting to train—clued me into the value of embracing and flowing with imperfection, on the mat and in life. In the first instance, when I didn't want to go, I actually ended up on the mat, with zero expectations. I was just there—even though I had convinced myself I didn't want to be. As a result, the outcome of that day didn't matter to me. Starting at "zero," I had everything to gain and nothing to lose. In the second scenario, by contrast, I had so many expectations there was no way I could ever live up to them on the mat. I was so hyped and primed for action, that when things didn't go the way I wanted or expected, I ended up becoming my own worst enemy. My inner-critic took over, as I scrambled and searched for the "right answers" in my head. On those days, I second-guessed everything I did. My mind was way too active, burning up all the energy that should have been released into the flow of my body in action.

The second and crucial lesson then is this: Just because you feel or think a certain way, it doesn't *have* to define the outcome. And coming back to what I wrote earlier, most of the time the key to peak performance is to simply get our thinking and judging minds out of the way, and allow the body to *feel our thinking*. In other words, make the crucial decisions we need to make, in order to succeed.

Beyond Positive Thinking

Rationally, I know that if I am feeling and thinking in a negative way about training, it makes sense to expect that I should have an awful experience. But experience has taught me this isn't always the case. This discovery flies in the face of what is typically stated in traditional psychological skills training (PST), a process often used in performance psychology. For example, typical PST training claims: "[The] reduction or control of negative thoughts, emotions, and bodily states and associated increases in confidence are directly related to the development of an ideal performance state." This "ideal performance state" is, in turn, believed to lead to the desired outcome of optimal performance."[2] Further, used as an intervention, it is assumed that PST, can effectively modify, or control, internal mental and emotional processes. In other words, according to theory, PST can enable people to:

---

[2] Hardy, L., Jones, G., & Gould, D. (1996). *Understanding Psychological Preparation for Sport: Theory and Practice of Elite Performers*. Wiley, Chichester.

- lower or suppress what are considered negative emotional states such as fear and anxiety;
- change negative thinking patterns to positive ones;
- relax instead of being over aroused.

Advocates of PST believe that these interventions ("positive thinking" and avoidance of "negative" emotions) are sufficient to lead to peak performance. However, decades of experience working on myself, and with many clients, have taught me otherwise. First of all, quite often, PST skills are developed off-field (e.g. in a classroom setting) with the hope that later they will be applied in practice, and, as a result, will then transfer over to the actual event they have been trained for. Some of the most common PST methods used for developing "mental game" performance include: visualization, positive thinking, positive affirmations, and relaxation techniques. The basic assumption behind PST training is, that knowledge gained from these practices will, with sufficient training and rehearsal, transfer over into the actual performance.

But, as noted, my experience flatly contradicts basic PST assumptions. On the contrary, over and over, I have witnessed, and personally experienced, how so-called positive thinking gets in the way of peak performance. So what's really going on?

In the first example, when I went to train not wanting to, I had no expectations. In the second example, when I was amped up, I had more expectations than I knew what do with. In the first instance, I unconsciously accepted what is; in the latter, I had filled my mind with expectations of what should be. In short, in one situation, I simply flowed with the reality presented to me, whether I liked it or not; while in the second, I resisted reality whenever it did not meet, or match, my expectations. Big difference. And, it explains a lot—particularly, a major blind spot in modern psychological skills training, often advocated by sport psychologists. The key here is this: More often than not, "positive thinking" amounts to a rejection of reality, a denial of what's so. And, in martial arts, as in just about any activity or circumstance, that's a recipe for disaster and disappointment.

As Nikos Kazantzakis, Greek writer and philosopher, reminds us: "Since we cannot change reality, let us change the eyes which see reality." That's what the next section is about.

Acceptance

By contrast, adopting or creating an attitude of *acceptance*—not positive thinking—is the most effective antidote to the stress often associated with uncertainty, and imperfection. Nowhere is this more beautifully stated than in the *Bhagavad Gita*, a core text in the Hindu religion: "It is better to live your own destiny imperfectly than to live an imitation of somebody else's life with perfection." We can learn an important lesson from the *wabi-sabi* of performance: To find the beauty in imperfection, one has to begin with acceptance.

Let me clarify a crucial distinction: "Acceptance" is not at all the same as "resignation." Resignation means giving up. Acceptance on the other hand, is first and foremost, about not resisting whatever presents itself (externally out in the world or internally inside our thinking mind). And it's more than that: It implies also a positive orientation to what is, by not resisting what is. With that attitudinal baseline, the next crucial component of acceptance is a willingness to take action regardless of how you might be feeling, or thinking, in that moment.

In short, my experience has taught me that there are three important overarching processes that need to be in play, in order to bring about peak performance experience, in sparring, or in life:

Mindfulness in action (embodied-mind presence and awareness);

Acceptance (trusting the body-mind to respond effectively to what's so);

Commitment (staying the course, no matter what thoughts or emotions arise in the midst of high-pressure encounters).

In *Deep Survival: Who Lives, Who Dies, and Why*, Laurence Gonzales discusses how, when confronted with a life-threatening situation, ninety percent of people freeze or panic, while only ten percent stay cool, focused—and alive.

Gonzales concludes that in order to live through a catastrophe, you have to accept pain and suffering (*acceptance*), if you're ever going to get out of it alive. You have to be absorbed completely in the present situation (*mindful*). You surrender to "what's so"—by adapting to, and engaging with, the new reality you find yourself in (*commitment*). In doing so, you will have a much better chance of surviving than someone who remains in denial, clinging to wishful or fearful thinking. Gonzales writes: "They [the survivors] are the ones who can perceive their situation clearly; they can plan and take correct action" (*commitment*).

These three core ingredients—acceptance, mindful attitude, and commitment—remain the same, whether sparring or living through a catastrophe. Both experiences require high performance under pressure—especially, when how you respond to the situation could mean the difference between life and death.

The truth is: Acceptance takes practice. And, you don't have to be thrown into a catastrophe to begin this practice. The best way to practice is to start small. Start with things you can change—no matter how minor or seemingly insignificant. When I first began training in Brazilian jiu-jitsu, a wrestling art, my coach Master Rigan Machado told me, during a moment when he saw I was frustrated at not being able to escape a specific position: "Success in jiu-jitsu is measured in seconds, not minutes." Ha!

He meant, of course: "Look you are stuck. You know the technique for how to escape, but you are still stuck. Now, the reasons could be many . . . you are not moving enough, your timing is off, etc. But just 'accept' where you are, and the more you practice escaping without becoming frustrated (mindfulness-in-action), and the more you decide to take action to change your situation (commitment), success is more likely to happen." When I finally did escape it took me five minutes. In time, I was able to shave off a few seconds.

That's when I had a light-bulb moment. My coach was pointing out that success is defined, not by a textbook escape that gets you immediately to your goal (i.e. getting it perfect every time); but rather, success involves incremental improvements over time. And this requires practice—putting yourself in the same bad position, over and over, and shaving off a few seconds each time you escape. Although I wasn't fully aware of it at the time, jiu-jitsu and my coach taught me to accept where I was, and then to take the necessary action steps, regardless of how small, to achieve future success.

This is where a lot of people go wrong: I see it happening frequently. Understandably, they don't like where they find themselves, and want to change it; but, because the problem seems so big, they feel the only way they can change it is by getting every move just perfect. They set unattainable goals, trying to accomplish the endgame in one move. They haven't yet realized that success is an incremental process. As the cliché goes: "The stars are never perfectly aligned." Waiting for everything to line up "just right" could take a long time, and in my experience it might never happen. Perfection may take an eternity, and that's not available to us mere, mortal humans—and certainly not when fighting on the mat, or tackling the challenges of day-to-day life are involved. Making incremental and sustainable change in the face of uncertainty, unpredictability, and chaos requires acceptance—seeing imperfection not as something scary, but as an opportunity to grow. That's *wabi-sabi*: Accepting the "perfection" of imperfection.

The Beauty of Mundane Imperfection

Building on the idea that success happens incrementally, not in a flash of brilliance, *wabi-sabi* speaks equally to the beauty of the mundane, the ordinary. David Byrne, a Scottish musician, and a founding member and principal songwriter of the American new wave band Talking Heads, noted: "Life tends to be an accumulation of a lot of mundane decisions, which often gets ignored."

Every day, we read about people achieving extraordinary results. Some climb Mt. Everest, others make their first few million dollars, or a top sports person wins a championship match. We admire these people, and rightfully so. They show all of us what the human spirit, our human potential, is capable of. We dream of our own potential too. If only we could make our mark on the world; if only we could have this kind of success in our own lives.

While remaining focused on the pinnacle of other people's amazing success, many are unconscious to the fact, that what really defines who we are, are not those exceptional moments of glory and achievement. Rather, what is rarely spoken of is the fact that success happens in the mundane, humdrum world of everyday actions. Most people spend so much time dreaming of the future they want, that they fail to realize that what truly shapes who they will become, is living exceptionally in the day-to-day grind, in every moment.

Most people don't know that every interaction they have, and how they react to it, day in and day out, especially in what is considered mundane—such as driving to work, dropping the kids off at school, or listening to the news—shapes who they will become, more than anything else they do with their lives. In other words, how you live in the imperfection of life, every moment, and the attitude you create about it, has a cumulative effect over time. This will either lead to true success, or failure. When we see someone who is successful, we don't see that their success is a culmination of what they did every step of the way that got them to the peak. Every adventurer who ever stood atop Mt. Everest, left a trail of footprints in the snow stretching back to base camp.

Every experience we have shapes our brain, whether we are conscious of it or not—especially repeated experiences. In my view, how you react to being stuck in morning traffic, is a far greater predictor of your future success than telling me about your dreams. Being stuck in traffic is something you likely experience every day. Bottom-line: Environment plays an essential role in shaping who you are. How you interact with that environment each day, is going to decide who you will ultimately become. If your default setting is road rage, day in and day out, that way of reacting to a mundane and imperfect experience (something we all endure) will shape you into someone set on a hair-trigger. Rather than "practice makes perfect," we can now see that a more accurate saying might be: *"Practice imperfection" (wabi-sabi)*—because if you don't, if you practice rage or anger (for example), every time things don't turn out as you want or expect them to, your resistance to life's inevitable imperfections will program your brain to automatically respond that way. And that's a recipe for an unhappy, unhealthy—and probably a short—life.

Second, what you do with your body—*how* you engage with adversity—also shapes your brain. Studies have shown that a person's self-esteem can be heightened by the simple act of making a fist. As a person's body adopts a protective, confident stance, their mind feels better able to focus on the problems at hand. How you show up in the world then, matters.

For example, let's take a familiar, mundane situation: As I walk around the mall, I see most people at work, standing behind the counter displaying a body attitude of, "I hate my job, and I don't want to be here." Going to work, every day is boring and mundane for them. They fail to realize that keeping their body in a constant state of, "I don't want to be here," doesn't just shape that moment of experience for them, but programs their future as well. By contrast, if you show up like it matters—not just today, but every day—even ordinary events and occupations can become extraordinary. How you show up today, will define how you show up later on in life.

Third, language changes your brain, too. In, *Words Can Change Your Brain*, Newberg and Waldman, wrote: "A single word has the power to influence the expression of genes that regulate physical and emotional stress." In other words (no pun intended), if you use positive language, it motivates you to see the world as positive, and if you use negative language, the world seems like a really bad place. How you talk to others, and to yourself matters, and will shape who you become in the future. However, let's be clear, this does not mean an endorsement of positive thinking (as in PST). All my earlier warnings and caveats still hold:

If "being positive" means suppressing authentic negative emotions, then all you are really doing is adding fuel to the fire of negativity burning in your belly. Rather than suppress fearful or angry emotions, it's far better to *notice* them, become *fully aware* of them as they arise, but don't let them take over your mind-body. Much better to have your emotions; than to let your emotions have you.

Nevertheless, it remains true that we always have a choice about the language we use to interpret or describe any situation we find ourselves in. Choosing to see and talk about "the glass half full" (or "half empty"), doesn't change the objective fact of the amount of water in the glass. But, it does change something in our brains so that the words we use to describe reality, can act like filters that color the world we experience. So, ditching positive thinking doesn't mean you shouldn't watch your language. For example, let's say you are in a fight and you feel trapped, afraid you might get beaten. The reality is you are experiencing fear. Telling yourself, "I'm not afraid," won't help you get out of your predicament. That will just disconnect you from reality, and magnify the chances you will lose. However, if you allow yourself to *feel the fear* without attaching negative words to it, such as, "He'll sense my fear and take advantage of it," and instead change your language to something like, "I can use my fear to motivate me," your brain will get the message and will be more likely to respond in ways that lead to a more desirable outcome.

How you react to the imperfections of the mundane world, every day—from how you think about being stuck in a queue at the store, to managing your emotions while caught in another traffic jam, or how you hold and present your body attitude at that job you are not fond of — is one of the most decisive predictors of your future success. Behavior is mediated by the brain and, vice versa, how we act, or behave, feeds back into the brain. The point is that, *how we choose* to live our day-to-day lives shapes this feedback loop between brain and body-mind. In simple terms, what changes the brain, changes who you are. You are sculpted not in one day, but by all the minor, mundane events, of a lifetime of experiences.

The good news: Change your behavior, and you can change your brain (much of what this book is about). Who you will become, will not be shaped by those once-in-a-while moments of glory and success—or what I call the *Braveheart* speech. No, who you are going to become, will be determined far less by the major dramas in your life, than by the little things—such as how you react in traffic today and tomorrow, or how you react with your body when you see someone jump the queue in the store. In other words, how you deal with the minor imperfections of daily living are your stepping stones to success (or failure).

We all need dreams. We all need to read inspirational stories to think big, to inspire us. But making it big doesn't happen in the "big" moments; it happens from all those small moments you would otherwise hardly notice. By all means hold big dreams and visions, shoot for the stars—but do so knowing, that getting there depends not on the dream, but on how you react to those inevitable times when someone or something gets in your way and threatens to shatter your dream. That's when your attitude and commitment to integrity, as you take every small, ordinary step toward your goal will guide you toward success. As Harvey Pekar, American underground comic book writer, music critic, and media personality reminds us: "As a matter of fact, I deliberately look for the mundane, because I feel these stories are ignored. The most influential things that happen to virtually all of us are the things that happen on a daily basis. Not the traumas.

And, taking the words of singer-songwriter Rufus Wainwright, to heart, the beauty of imperfection lies in making "the mundane fabulous whenever [you] can."

Accepting Imperfection Doesn't Mean Being Lazy

As a coach, I hear a lot of people talk about what they need to do in order to become successful. A year or more later, I meet the same people, who still find themselves in the same place they were years earlier. Clearly, there seems to be a disconnect between what people say they want, and what people need to do to make it happen. Much of this follows from what I have written in previous paragraphs.

People want things to be just right, to be perfect, before they decide to make their move. As I have outlined, perfection is really an illusion. One has to come to peace with the fact that nothing will ever be perfect—on the mat, or in the ring, or in life. Accepting this, however, doesn't mean being resigned to failure. Too many people use the imperfection of life, or career, as an excuse: "Look, life has it in for me. I just cannot do it." Or they sit back and hope success will just come to them. But, as serial entrepreneur, wine enthusiast, and social media wiz Gary Vaynerchuk would say: You cannot have success without the hustle.

While it is important to have a goal, an end destination, success happens in every step of the journey. Hardly ever does one single event lead to success; rather, it takes a series of small, everyday hustles in the midst of the mundane, imperfect events of life to achieve success. This is why successful people almost never point to a single moment that turned the tide. Instead, they describe the day-today hustle, working incrementally, moment by moment, steadfastly moving passionately toward their goals—even when they didn't feel life was on their side. That, ultimately, is the "secret" of success.

People don't lack success because they don't have a good idea, or a noble dream; they don't achieve success because, they don't want to work on their idea, or dream, every moment of every day. Put simply: They don't want to hustle. If you habitually moan about life's imperfection every time you have to work on an idea—including, and especially, the boring or difficult stuff—forget it, because you have already just about guaranteed you will not succeed.

As Gary Vaynerchuk notes: "The reason I was able to grow my business was that every day, after producing 30 minutes of wine television, I spent 15 hours a day replying to every single person's e-mail and every single person's Twitter @ reply."

Sadly, people want those *Braveheart* speech moments—the highs, the applause, the recognition, the lights—but they don't want to go to battle. Being truly successful at anything isn't won in the speech; it's won in the day-to-day battle, the hustle. It's won by how you engage with every mundane moment, the unimportant stuff; it is won when you work toward your goals, when almost everything around you seems imperfect, or even stacked against you.

You can win the hard battle of life by being smart, resourceful, and committed to success—no matter what obstacles get thrown in your way. Here are my top five tips for being smart about how to engage in the hustle:

Be prepared to do the work. No excuses. I'm sorry, as simple as it may sound; there is no substitute for hard work. Make sure you are passionate about your idea or goal, because if you are not, you simply won't do the daily work required to transform it into a success.

Working hard is not a substitute for working smart. Get a system going (the six principles I outline in this book make a great system). Figure out what is critical for making what you want happen. Break it into smaller chunks, and assign specific times and days to work on it. Even if it means you can only do it at 10 PM at night. Then do it, even if you don't feel like it (although, as pointed out in principle #1, that's already a problem).

Consistency is far more important than quantity. It's not how much you do; it is how often you do it, and do it well. Doing a small amount of important quality work on your success plan every day, is far more important than putting in long hours of work once in a while. Remember, it's how you deal with the day-to-day hustle that leads to success.

Get inspired to hustle. Find people who you admire, people who know how to turn the hustle into success. Watch them, listen to them, read their words and take notes. Then feed those notes into your system (see point #2). When you finally start getting some traction—when people begin to listen to what you have to say— nurture those relationships. Be consistent. Honor their attention. Be respectful of their time. Don't try to sell them stuff. Instead, ask what you can do for them—and *listen*.

When you finally see the success on the horizon, and even when it arrives, keep your feet firmly on the ground. Most important: *Don't get lazy!* I call it the "Rocky Syndrome." If you have watched the *Rocky* movies, you will remember that when the character Rocky Balboa was hungry, when he was passionate, when he did that punishing run every day (even when he didn't want to), he finally succeeded. But, a few movies later, once he had "arrived" and had all the trappings of success, he didn't hustle anymore. Big mistake.

As Rocky (Sylvester Stallone) reminds us: "Let me tell you something you already know. The world ain't all sunshine and rainbows. It's a very mean and nasty place, and I don't care how tough you are it will beat you to your knees and keep you there permanently if you let it. You, me, or nobody is gonna hit as hard as life. But it ain't about how hard ya hit. It's about how hard you can get it and keep moving forward. How much you can take and keep moving forward. That's how winning is done! Now if you know what you're worth then go out and get what you're worth. But ya gotta be willing to take the hits, and not pointing fingers saying you ain't where you wanna be because of him, or her, or anybody! Cowards do that and that ain't you! You're better than that!"

An Imperfection Work-Around: Focus on Strengths

From a young age, we are taught to strive, to work harder, and be better. Everything from Disney movies, to the American Dream reinforces the idea, "If you dream it, you can achieve it"—as long as you are willing to work for it. But how realistic is this?

Can we really always get what we want if we just invest a little more time, and put in the elbow grease to make it happen?

You may have heard that if you work to improve your weaker areas, you can be successful and accomplish your goals. This weakness-fixing perspective is prevalent in many cultures, especially those that encourage a strong work-ethic and self-discipline to get a job done. Based on this mindset, many people blame their failures on a lack of personal effort, claiming that if they had just worked a little harder, they could have been successful. And this mindset is reinforced when we get negative feedback at work, or criticized for the things we've done poorly in our relationships and families.

Now, contrast this mentality with a strengths-building perspective. According to a survey of more than two million people,[3] Gallup researchers discovered, that while weakness-fixing can prevent failure, strength-building makes a decisive difference that actually leads to success in the short- and long-term. The data suggests that while we can develop certain skills through hard work, we all have some skills, or aptitudes, that naturally come easier because of our personal strengths.

Working from a position of weakness, while striving to be your best, is like signing your name with your non-dominant hand. It's unnatural, messy, and often frustrating, or even stress-inducing. Yet, so often we continue to pour time and energy into these areas of weakness, just to improve a little bit. However, the resources at our disposal—time, energy, money, etc.—are finite, and we can only do so much to improve before we get burnt out, or frustrated.

It doesn't help that most of us are told from a young age, that we need to develop our skills to be "well-rounded." Sadly, this often results in us forcing ourselves to try and perfect things where our natural talents do not lie. Alex Linely, Director of the Centre for Applied Positive Psychology, labels the phenomenon of trying to perform well in almost every area of life, the "Curse of Mediocrity."[4]

---

[3] Buckingham, M. & Clifton, D. O. (2001). *Now, discover your strengths.* New York: The Free Press.
[4] Linley, A. (2008). Average to A+: realising strengths in yourself and others. Coventry, UK: CAPP Press.

When you're trying to be good in everything, you end up being great at nothing. It's like the popular saying: "Jack of all trades, master of none."

If you're still a little skeptical about all this, you're not alone. Most people take a problem-focused approach to life, spending their time, energy, and money, fixing things that aren't right, instead of maximizing the things that are. And in many cultures, focusing on your strengths may be perceived as arrogant or self-absorbed.

Below, I list some reasons why we don't look at our strengths:[5]

- We are not always aware of our strengths.
- Even when we are aware of them, we often don't get feedback on our strengths.
- We are encouraged to be humble based on social norms.
- We may not have opportunities to use our strengths.
- The problems we face are too pressing, or require too urgent a response, that they don't allow us time to develop or apply our strengths.
- We think that our areas of weakness are our best potential for growth.

But, where do we get the biggest bang for our buck? Both research and personal experience show that our strengths, not our weaknesses, bring us the biggest returns. You can tell when you are working from a position of strength, by the burst of energy you gain from the activity. Just like working from areas of weakness, going against your strengths is uncomfortable, and requires a huge

---

[5] Biswas-Diener, R. (2010). *Practicing positive psychology coaching: Assessment, activities, and strategies for success.* Hoboken, New Jersey: John Wiley & Sons, Inc.

investment of energy. Imagine the radical changes you could make, just by shifting your attention away from concentrating on fixing your weaknesses, and instead investing that same energy into developing areas of potential strength to achieve personal mastery. That's how you uncover the proverbial "pot of gold."

At this point, I invite you to consider what it would be like to work from your strengths, and do what you do best every day. How would this impact your performance?

Research also shows, that people who use their strengths, more embody the following qualities:[6]

- They are happier.
- They are more confident.
- They have higher levels of self-esteem.
- They have higher levels of energy and vitality.
- They experience less stress.
- They are more resilient.
- They are more likely to achieve their goals.
- They perform better, and are more engaged at work.
- They are more effective at developing themselves, and growing as individuals.

These same qualities show up not just at work, but in all aspects of life, when we focus on developing our strengths. That's how we enhance our performance,

---

[6] Linley, A., Willars, J., & Biswas-Diener, R. (2010). *The strengths book: Be confident, be successfully, and enjoy better relationships by realising the best of you.* Coventry, UK: CAPP Press.

and overall life satisfaction. Adopting a strengths-based approach to work, and life, doesn't mean you should give up on improving your weaknesses entirely. In fact, ignoring your weaknesses is a huge liability when working on improving your strengths. If you don't attend to your weak areas and focus only on your strengths, those weaknesses will trip you up as you strive to move forward.

Think of it as another aspect of life-balance. If you view your weaknesses as *yin,* and your strengths as *yang,* then the optimum state to aim for is a dynamic balance between your *yin* and *yang.* By working on your strengths, you will grow in ability and confidence, and this will help you tackle your weaknesses more effectively. By improving your weak areas, you build up resources, and skills that will help you develop your strengths even further. However, begin by identifying your strengths and work on developing those first. Once you've built up some level of accomplishment (no matter how small), it will build confidence when you turn your attention to working on your weaknesses.

Remember: Take it step-by-step. Be patient. Don't try to build the Great Wall of China in one day, or even a few months. Focus on crafting a single "brick," and then another, and then another . . . and soon, before you know it, you will already have started building your own *Great Wall* (whatever that translates to in your life). As always, the decisive difference comes from your commitment to tackling life's mundane activities and chores with persistence and impeccability.

A strengths-building approach helps us make conscious choices about where we want to invest our energy to get the results we desire. It's all about personal choice, and the actions that follow. While it might be tempting to work on improving your weaker areas first, which can help you from losing in the short run, the sure and steady path to winning in the long run, is to maximize your strengths.

Reflective Exercises

Let's round up this chapter with a few questions to kick start your path to *wabi-sabi,* to seeing the *"beauty in imperfection"*:

- What imperfection most hinders your growth? (Describe only one or two).
- Describe the fear that this creates, and how it immobilizes you.
- Describe at least three actions you will take, beginning today, to move beyond your fear of this imperfection (remember, small steps count).
- Describe how changing your perception of this imperfection can motivate, and mobilize, you.

In the end, as my friend John Michael Morgan, author of *Brand Against The Machine,* has noted: "If you're waiting for things to be perfect before you start chasing your dream, then get comfortable . . . you're gonna be here awhile."

Principle 2

Buddha Mind, Warrior Body

"What we achieve inwardly will change outer reality."

—Plutarch

A focused mind leads to a focused life. Remember, throughout this book, I am talking about real performance, in the heat of the battle—whether in the ring where your opponent is intent on knocking you out, or in the corporate world where your competition tries to score a knockout deal at your expense. The quality of your performance happens in that very moment of negotiation, and makes the difference between winning and losing. Bottom line: Whenever you have to take action to achieve success, you need to act *in the moment,* not at some future time—an hour, a day, a month away. In fact, in many situations—especially in the ring, but also in the boardroom—delaying action, even for a split second, can make or break success. Peak performance happens *now*—always now, never at any other time. Doing well here requires a very different approach.

In the previous chapter, I discussed the beauty of imperfection, *wabi-sabi.* In life, we become most aware of imperfection when we realize that everything—including us and our loved ones—is *impermanent.* And, furthermore, impermanence is often coupled with *uncertainty.* Whether in life, or on the mat, we have to face the fact that nothing ever stays the same for long, that everything changes, and, for the most part, we can never know for certain what's going to happen next. Life is always in flux, a series of fleeting, unpredictable moments. That, then, is the source of our sense of imperfection. How perfect life would be *if only* we knew for certain we would live forever, and that the things and people we love would never change, grow old, or die.

But is that really true? Think about it: If nothing ever changed, if everything was perfectly predictable, how boring would that be? Nothing would ever grow. Life would lack all contrast and dynamism. Creativity would be frozen in stone. Instead of living in a state of wishful thinking, peppering our lives with a string of "if onlys," a "perfect" life embraces the transitoriness of existence, its novelty and unpredictability—its "imperfection." This insight lies at the heart of Buddhism, one of the world's oldest and greatest spiritual philosophies.

So, with that in mind, let's dive into this chapter by accepting that everything is impermanent, and unpredictable, and learning to see that as a cause for celebration. The best way to achieve success—in fact, the *only* way—is to stop resisting reality. The simple fact is that everything is always changing, and we often don't know what's coming next. This is as true in the dojo, on the mat, as it is through the thick and thin of the rest of life.

Many people get anxious when faced with uncertainty, and so, they try to organize their lives to minimize risk. However, in doing so, they close down all kinds of opportunities that might otherwise open up for them. Nevertheless, you don't want to throw all caution to the wind, and steamroll ahead, diving into every risky situation that comes you way. That would be silly (think of the wild ways of adolescents, and you get an idea of what I'm talking about). No, a certain amount of risk-taking adds spice to life, creates new options, and makes life interesting. Some degree of risk is also necessary to succeed in the grand adventure of life. But instead of diving in head first, blindly pushing ahead without paying attention to the lay of the land, a much wiser course of action, is to develop specific tools and techniques that will help you navigate through the transitoriness, and unpredictability, of life. That's what we'll look at in this chapter: "Buddha Mind, Warrior Body." Alternatively, we could call it "Buddha Mind, Warrior Heart" because while cultivating the peace and equilibrium of a "buddha mind," it's also important to develop the attitude (both mental and embodied) of a warrior—the warrior's "heart."

One of the first things I discovered in fighting is that my thinking mind can get in my way. Thinking itself isn't inherently bad, but what we focus on can be. In sparring, in a fight—indeed, any situation where split-second action is decisive—projecting thoughts into the future, or holding onto the past, will trip you up. There's a time for planning (future-oriented thinking) and a time for analyzing or evaluating what has happened (past-oriented thinking); but, when what really counts is what is happening *now,* you need to discipline your mind to *stay present,* and not get sidetracked into future- or past-thinking.

The reason for this is simple enough, a piece of common-sense philosophy: Ask yourself the following question: *"When does reality happen?"* Well, quite obviously, it always happens *now,* never at any other time. Reality does not happen in the past (that's already gone, over and done with, and never to be relived). Nor does reality happen in the future because, by definition, the future does not yet exist. (If the future *did* exist, it would not be the "future," it would be part of the present.) So, the only time reality, anything, ever happens, is *right now.*

Okay, now ask yourself: *"When does experience happen?"* Again, and for similar reasons, the answer is also *right now.* In other words, both reality, and your experience of reality, always happens in the present moment. Now, a third question: *"When do you act?"* Once again, it's clear that every action always happens *right now,* in the present moment. You can't act on or in the past (because that's already a done deal), and you can't act in the future (because it doesn't yet exist).

Therefore, it follows, that if you want to engage with reality *as it is* (which is what you have to do if you want any kind of mastery), you have to keep your mind focused on the present. You need to pay attention to *whatever* you happen to be experiencing *right now.* When you do that, your in-the-moment experience guides your actions to meet reality exactly where it is. Your actions and reality coincide—and that's the most important foundation for taking masterful action—for peak performance.

On the other hand, if you let your mind wander off into judgments about some past event (whether just a moment ago or many moons ago), or into planning or fantasy about some future moment (whether just a second or two from now or some more remote time yet to come), you decouple yourself from reality, and your actions will inevitably be out of sync with what's required in the moment.

Now, this doesn't mean you should chastise yourself if you notice you are worrying about the future, or wishing you had done something different in the past. That kind of mental activity is natural for us humans. Our minds are prone to wander. In fact, they evolved to do just that.

But, when you begin to cultivate what I call "buddha mind," you don't get sucked into your thoughts; you don't let them derail you from the present moment—at least not for long. As soon as you realize your mind is wandering, you make a choice to refocus your attention back into the present moment. By all means *notice* when your mind wanders, just don't let it seduce you into some story about what just happened, or about what might happen next. Buddha mind *is* present mind.

When your thoughts are hooked into the past, or the future, your mind is not attending to the actual experience you are having right now. Rather, it is about what just happened a moment ago, or what you anticipate will happen in the next second. When your thoughts are moving into the past or the future, you can easily get caught up in the mental vortex, and spin out of control.

If you want to get yourself into trouble quickly in sparring (or at work when you need to perform at your peak), start thinking about what an opponent is about to do next, or hold onto what he just did to you. In either case, the outcome will be the same, you will lose touch with the present moment—the here and now—the only place, and time, true performance ever happens. In the ring, the consequences of a wandering mind can be immediate and painful—you get punched in the face. In business deals, a wandering mind takes your attention off important aspects of the negotiation, and you get suckered. The time for planning and analyzing is *before* the negotiation; the time for evaluation comes *after*. The present moment requires your full participating, embodied presence *in the present moment*. It's a simple as that. Nowhere is this idea more evident than in the writings of the Samurai, ancient Japanese warriors. Closely connected to Zen Buddhism, the Samurai cultivated an exceptional sense of timing, and a feeling for the beauty of impermanence and imperfection—*wabi-sabi*. This is what it meant to be a Samurai warrior. We might even call it the art or aesthetics of being a warrior.

In the *Unfettered Mind*, Takuan Soho, who fused the art of swordsmanship with Zen ritual wrote: "The mind that becomes fixed and stops in one place does not function freely. Similarly, the wheels of a cart go around because they are not held rigidly in place. If they were to stick tight, they would not go around. The mind is also something that does not function if it becomes attached to a single situation."

The opposite of a fixed mind, Takuan called, "no-mind." Fixed mind, then, is a mind caught up in thoughts about the future, or the past. Instead of paying attention to what is actually happening *now,* the thinking mind gets fixated on some imaginary future, or some irretrievable past. Either way, the thinking mind stops being anchored in the present. In that sense, then, it is not "true mind," as Takuan would suggest. He also points out that true mind, or no-mind, is not getting tangled up in the intellect, getting "into your head." Instead, "no-mind" is not the complete absence of consciousness, but, quite the contrary, it refers to awareness that encompasses the entire body without discrimination, and extends to the entire self. It is what I have referred to in this book, as "embodied-mind." In other words, no-mind is not hindered, or fixed, in one place (past or future) and is instead free to act when, and where, it is needed. In a word: No-mind is a fluid mind.

In martial arts, to have no-mind is to be grounded, fully present in our body. When you achieve groundedness, you embody a felt sense of being, that is in touch with all aspects of your reality. This includes your thoughts, emotions, sensations, and the experience that is happening now—all deeply felt and connected with your body.

The question then arises: How do you achieve this?

Ask anyone to stop thinking, and they simply can't. Thinking happens all the time, whether we want to or not. The trick then, is to use thinking to one's advantage. Rather than trying to eradicate thinking, which you simply cannot achieve, you can use your mind to refocus awareness back to the present moment. It's like fine-tuning a radio, getting past all the static and locating a specific, clear radio station. Do it right, and you will be greeted by: "Welcome to radio NOW!" Once you have your thinking mind back in the present, you can let it go, sit back, and enjoy the music.

Before I go any further, I want to make something clear: I am not advocating that past- or future-based thinking is wrong, or that you shouldn't do it. Without this kind of thinking, you wouldn't be able to learn from past mistakes, and you wouldn't be able to plan for the future. Both forms of thinking are necessary to live a full, happy, and healthy life. However, when you need to perform, in the heat of the battle, when the chips are on the table, you absolutely *have* to be present. There is no way, you can attend to what needs to be done in the moment of peak performance, if your attention is not focused right here, right now.

Second, and crucially, I tell all my clients on the mat, that in the heat of the moment when you are expected to bring your "A" game, that is not the time to start planning. You either have what it takes to face that moment, or you don't. Training and planning should happen *before* an actual performance, before a do-or-die event, not during it.

Here is the paradox: In order to be prepared for peak performance, you need to do your training in a similar, and closely related, circumstance. For example, if you want to train for a fight, then *practice while in the ring, or on the mat.* Don't practice in situations that don't match what you will have to actually deal with. Such practice might help you get fit, but it won't help you fine-tune the skills you will need, when, as they say, "the rubber hits the road." In other words, the best time to practice being present, is in the heat of the moment, when you are likely to experience the kinds of anxieties, fears, or other emotions that will be triggered during the actual event. Obviously, you don't have to exactly duplicate the environment or circumstances (in fact, that's impossible): But, you do want to practice in circumstances that resemble, as closely as possible, the event you are training for. This makes it more real, concrete, and specific. When the crucial moment comes, success (or failure) will not be only in your head—you will *embody* it. In my experience, just knowing you can do something is not enough; you need to trust, with your *entire* body-mind, that you can take on the challenge. This unshakable confidence is a vital component for you to succeed. So, for example, in martial arts you need to practice being present *during sparring itself*; you need to mirror, as best you can, the actual peak performance event you are training for. You won't get what you need for success by sitting on a zafu, or meditation cushion.

Now, I know this can be scary, especially if the event you are training for is high pressure, with serious consequences if you make a mistake. Take leaders, for example. I work with a lot of leaders, but, for most of them the only opportunity to practice skills related to leadership performance, is in the crucible of work, where often their actions could have real, substantial consequences. In that case, most leaders would prefer, at least initially, to practice what I teach about performance not on the job (where too much might be at risk), but during offsite training sessions with me. Then, as they begin to embody the skills necessary for peak performance, they can later incorporate them into the pressure-cooker of the workplace. I have developed special martial arts-based programs for leaders (in corporate, sports, and law-enforcement environments), designed to increase their levels of embodied self-awareness that enable them to experience peak performance during times of high-stress—but in a safe container.

Unlike in their professional day-to-day work, as they practice these somatic skills in my studio, they can pause, ask questions, troubleshoot, or reset when and wherever needed. This gives them an opportunity to iron out rough edges, before applying these techniques at work. Having developed a satisfactory degree of mind-body skill via martial arts, it then becomes much easier for leaders to transfer that knowledge to the actual work environment.

Now, although martial arts' training is not directly related to leadership *per-se*, many of the mental challenges leaders encounter on the training mat (e.g. acting with clarity and intent in the face of stress, anxiety, or fear, and thinking on their feet), are similar to the kinds of stress, and other mental challenges, that they face in their professional lives. For example, quick decision-making, especially in a crisis, is a prized leadership quality. The outcome of these decisions can impact organizational strategy or structure, and affect the business bottom-line, one way or the other.

Training on the mat in an intense sparring episode, gives them first-hand experience of needing to make quick decisions—in this case, about how to move, how to integrate mind and body, how to manage emotions, how to remain mentally clear and observant, and to know when it's best to defend, or attack. In martial arts training, leaders learn to recognize an open target, and how to engage it with accuracy. Both in effective martial arts and leadership, a leader's attitude, cognitive-emotional dynamics, embodied-intelligence and self-control, *right at the crucial moment of decision* can make the difference between getting "hit" and striking a winning blow. In short, the embodied-mind performance practice of martial arts, offers leaders a pressure-cooker opportunity, to instinctively know how to act from an embodied experience of peak performance. As you will have gathered by now: One of the core skills needed for successful leadership— and in any area of life—is the ability to *be fully present in the moment* even, or especially, when the proverbial "brown stuff" hits the fan. That's when quick and accurate decisions really count.

The key, then, is to find places in your life—on or off the mat—where you can practice the techniques outlined in this book. The "trick," of course, is to find an environment where the pressure is on, but not so intense that making a mistake could mean getting knocked out, or losing your job. You need the opportunity to practice, and to build confidence. Developing what I call an "embodied-mind performance game" is like learning any skill: It takes time, patience, and practice. The more you apply these skills to the smaller, daily challenges you face, the more you will be able to take on any major obstacles you will face later on. I can sum up the main teaching tool in this chapter in four words: *learn to ground your thoughts*. (Okay, I know that's five words; but, the essentials are "learn," "grounding" and "thoughts." By "grounding your thoughts," I mean finding way to be present, *embodied*, in the moment, when it really counts. My friend, colleague, and philosopher Dr. Christian de Quincey calls this, "feeling your thinking." He means paying attention to whatever is happening in your body from moment-to-moment, and noticing how your body's sensations inform, shape, and trigger your thoughts. One way to achieve this is through using what I call "re-focus strategies"—and that's what we will look at next.

Re-Focus Strategies

Re-focus strategies are action steps that you can take to achieve one specific goal—to remain *present* in the midst of peak performance. They help you remain focused on the experience at hand, in order to be fully present in the midst of a peak performance event. They enable you to get a handle on your mind, and to stop it from wandering, getting sucked into a sequence of thoughts irrelevant to the task at hand.

Re-focus strategies can be either, a *mental* routine that brings the thinking mind back to the present, or an *embodied* physical action, such as an anchoring technique, that allows the thinking mind to re-focus onto an immediate cue; thus giving you the opportunity to become present again in your thinking. I'll say more about "anchoring" later on. But for now, think of it like a kind of strategic "hook" that latches you onto, or brings you back to, the present moment.

I want to emphasize again, that thinking as such, is not the enemy of peak performance; the issue is more *what* you are thinking about, and whether your thoughts are directed at the past, future, or the present. The time for thinking—weighing up pros and cons, and analyzing the situation—is not when you are in the heat of action. That's when your thinking mind can derail you. As mentioned earlier, the time for thinking (planning), comes *before* the moment of action, and the time for evaluating comes *after.* As every artist (martial or aesthetic) knows: Thinking is the enemy of spontaneity. And this leads to another subtle, but important, distinction: The difference between "spontaneity" and "autopilot."

Being on "autopilot" means you think and act unconsciously, mechanically, as if you were a machine. You are not aware of what's happening, either in your mind, or your body. You are not present, no one's home. By contrast, being "spontaneous," couldn't be more different. First, spontaneous thinking or acting is conscious, in the sense of being *intentional*—you are fully present, you know what you are doing, and you are aware of what's going on in your body, and your mind. Second, whatever thoughts are passing through your mind don't get in your way—because *you have your thoughts,* you don't let them *have you.*

Third, when you act spontaneously, you act from *choice.* You let your intentions, not your thoughts, guide your actions. Setting an intention, begins with a choice, that then guides or orients what you do next—for example, creating the intention to achieve a goal, whether it's striking your opponent on the mat, or striking a business deal in the office. When you act on autopilot, however, you act out of *habit,* mechanically. *You are out of the picture,* and as a result your thoughts can, and usually do, run wild, taking you into the stormy waters of the past or the future.

Without mindfulness training, most people think on autopilot. Their mind wanders. It might sound like a contradiction, but in general, people are unconscious about their own thoughts. You can test this easily enough. Just ask a few people what they were thinking about a minute or two ago. Most likely, if they are honest, they will tell you they haven't a clue. Or, if they do have some faint memory of where their thoughts were focused, they won't be able to remember what led up to those particular thoughts. For most people, then, their thoughts *just happen,* as if someone, or something, else was behind the scenes tugging away at the strings of cognition. They are on autopilot, like a puppet on a string. The term "autopilot," then, can be defined as a state of mind in which one acts without conscious intention or awareness of present-moment sensory perception.

And that's why my "re-focus strategies" are important: They allow you to shift from a state of autopilot, a wandering mind, to *thinking on purpose.* Re-focus strategies are aimed at intentionally disengaging from autopilot, by bringing your attention back to the actuality of the moment, where the quality of your performance makes the difference. Using this method of re-focusing, you purposefully bring yourself back to the present moment, where you let go of your thoughts and let your body-mind's natural intelligence spontaneously guide your action in the moment. Achieving peak performance, on the mat, or elsewhere, requires this degree of focus.

The objective, then, of the re-focus strategies is to be present, and not be distracted by the past, or the future. The closer you can align with the present, connected to the correct body attitude (see Principle 3 below), the better your performance will be—whether in the boxing ring, or the ring of life.

Developing Re-Focus Mental Routines

Re-focus *cues* (the elements of each re-focus strategy) are special routines you can learn, in order to enhance peak performance. These cues can come in the form of purposefully learned implicit statements, and can help you re-focus attention back to the present moment. I probably need to unpack that mouthful: "Purposefully learned implicit statements." It might sound like jargon, but it actually expresses a simple fact.

The re-focus cues are "implicit" in the sense that each one could be a single word, or a simple phrase, that packs a lot of meaning and can quickly re-focus attention. They are "learned statements" in the sense that you train your body-mind to respond to them by repeating them many times while training for a performance event. These cues should be general and neutral, though they do need to be "purposeful," that is, relevant to the task at hand. For example, after years of coaching martial arts, I came to the conclusion that a few overarching re-focus cues are required for effective sparring, especially when one finds oneself in trouble. In general, this re-focus strategy (and its cohort of cues) involves balance, ensuring defense is active, backed up by tightly executed techniques, and a consistent focus on breath.

When sparring, I have learned to use the following cues to help me refocus quickly (these are simple words I silently repeat to myself): "Balance," "defense," "tight," and "breath." All I have to do is say these four words to myself, and immediately my body-mind responds appropriately and effectively; causing my reaction times to improve, so that I react faster to changing circumstances. Remember, I have trained these cue words in the midst of sparring, over and over again, progressively over time.

A single cue word can encapsulate a lot of meaning. That's its conceptual purpose: To bring a series of principles or techniques together, under one overarching idea. For example, saying "balance" to myself brings my focus into the present, because I know that balance is about feeling how my entire body-mind is oriented in that moment. While I might have trained specific techniques previously—like keeping a compacted stance and not crossing my feet—my cue word encapsulates all of these techniques into one phrase.

Besides "balance," other cues I use include "hands moving" (referring to active defense), "tight" (referring to tight economical structure, or body stance) and "breath." These all share a common trait: They are all "time neutral," meaning they are not tied to any future sparring expectations, or about holding onto a past experience. Re-focus cues have to be present tense. If they are tied to the past, or the future, they become *irrelevant* focus cues, or, to be more precise, they become *defocus* cues, because they split our focus, blurring our awareness of what is happening *right now*.

The following are some examples of past- or future-oriented cue words you need to stay away from:

Let's say I took a hit, and then murmured to myself, "I just got hit. Damn. I have to remember to move my hands next time, otherwise that will happen again." While this thought does include a positive re-focus cue, "hands moving," it contaminates, or neutralizes, the cue because it is both past- and future-focused. Because of this, it would not be considered an effective re-focus cue, at all.

Let's get clear on what we are trying to achieve by using a thinking-based re-focus strategy. As already noted, the thinking mind has a tendency to move between past- and future-based thinking. In other words, it wanders. It's in its nature to do so. Research shows that when we more or less accurately predict what someone is going to say, our brain activity is similar to theirs. In other words, our brains evolved to be prediction machines, constantly anticipating events in the world around us so that we can respond to them quickly and accurately. As far as survival goes, that's a good thing. However, a problem arises when we get bogged down in prediction, and stay there. We disconnect from the present, and hand our brains over to another form of autopilot.

In order to use re-focus strategies, you first have to identify that you are off task. This takes training in somatic self-awareness. Developing the skill to notice the moment you move into past- or future-based thinking, is crucial. If you are not aware that you have "vacated" your body-mind, you won't even know that you need to do something to bring yourself back to the present. But once you notice your mind wandering off target (the present), using your re-focus strategies returns you to your body-mind. Again, the process starts by noticing when you are anchored in either past- or future-based thinking. After some practice, you will come to recognize that your wandering mind often takes the form of a running narrative. We tend to spin stories, and get caught up in an inner dialogue *about* our performance, rather than spontaneously engaging in the action.

Back to the example I used earlier: "I just got hit. Damn. I have to remember to move my hands next time, otherwise that will happen again." First, notice the inner narrative: I was telling myself a story about what just happened, and, what I think might happen next. Then, notice that the narrative has different parts. One, I recognize that I got hit: Two, I remind myself to move my hands (a good thing)—experience has taught me that if I don't move my hands I'm likely to get hit again. On the face of it, there might seem to be nothing much wrong with having this internal dialogue—except for the most crucial part: *Reality*. In reality, someone is right there in front of me, trying to hit me in the face. The more I attend to the internal narrative, the more I am unable to attend to what is happening right now in the moment.

When we get lost in our stories, we lose contact with the present moment; and the present is the only time your opponent is trying to hit you. He is not going to stop hitting you, while you get you defense back together. In fact, more than likely, when he sees you struggling, he will probably seize the opportunity and strike a decisive blow. In my example, the longer I stay with the internal narrative, "I just got hit. Damn. I have to remember to move my hands next time..." the more I will get hit. I will have lost contact with the reality of the immediate environment that I need to deal with. In times of pressure and stress, the more we get "into our heads," into our stories, the more likely we will get knocked around. This applies not only while sparring on the mat, but also in any aspect of *full-contact living*.

Here is another example: How many times have you been in conversation with someone and, while they were talking, you were rehearsing, planning, a response in your head, only to suddenly realize that you had lost track of what the person was saying? When you do respond, it is likely to be out of context, disconnected from the actual point of the conversation.

Here's another useful distinction: We *react* to our stories rooted in past- or future-thinking; but we *respond* spontaneously when we are fully present and engaged. Reaction is mechanical (autopilot), and often inappropriate. Response is intentional, purposeful, and much more likely to be appropriate.

Once again, reflecting on the past or planning for the future isn't inherently bad; but it's bad when you have to be completely right here, right now. If you are a climber, standing on the edge of a rock face, three hundred meters off the ground, without a safety harness, that is not the time to start second-guessing yourself about where you should, or should not, place your hands next.

Let's call past- and future-based thinking, a cognitive "time-warp," because that's really what it is. It warps our sense of time and, more important, our sense of *timing*. Time-warp thinking, then, is all about second guessing yourself. And it's understandable because when it happens, it's an attempt to come to grips with what is going wrong. We then try to fix what just went wrong, or might go wrong in the next moment, we effectively (or ineffectively) pre-empt the outcome. In a peak performance environment such as sparring, trying to anticipate and set up a response before you even know what to respond to, can be disastrous. You have to respond, instead, to what is actually happening in the moment. In order to do this, you have to be right here, right now, completely present.

Okay, now that we've unpacked the problems with "time-warp" thinking, let's get back to our discussion on re-focus strategies. What they allow you to do, in summary, once you recognize that you are off task (either in the past or the future), is to anchor yourself back into the present moment. In this case, you are purposefully using your thinking mind to short-circuit its tendency to shift into story. Instead of getting lost in your narrative, you get back in touch with your body. You anchor yourself back in the present. Bottom line: It's *how* you use your thinking mind that matters. Let your thinking mind use you, and you're lost in a time-warp. However, use your thinking mind to pull yourself out of the story, back into the present moment . . . and you've got the essence of any re-focus strategy.

"I just got hit. Damn. I have to remember to move my hands next time, otherwise that will happen again."

Time-warp narratives like this are bound to take you out of the flow, and make you more vulnerable to attack. However, this example also highlights the value of re-focusing. Let's say you got hit while spinning this story, and then found yourself thinking about the fact that you just got hit, and immediately recognized in that moment that you were no longer present. That's a perfect time for you to use a re-focus cue word (e.g. "breath," "balance," "hands moving," or anything else that pulls your attention back into your body). Re-focusing your attention like this brings you back to the present. It liberates you from the grip of your story, and you are no longer attached to what just happened (getting hit). Instead, your re-focus strategy actively re-engages you in the moment, and that's when you have your best shot at regaining the upper hand.

Creating Your Own Cues

"Hands moving" is a time-neutral self-statement, or cue, that I came up with to help me re-focus. It works for me because it is not tied to the past or the future. It is something I simply say to myself in the present. It helps keep me in the *now*. However, just because these cues work for me doesn't mean they will work the same for you.

Here's a little exercise to help you come up with your own set of cues: Think about a performance-critical situation where you tend to struggle. Now write down what you see as the crucial elements needed to tackle the situation. Think back to some of your best performances: What did you do that allowed you to achieve success? Write down whatever comes to mind. Then think of one or two words, which encapsulate the essence, of that moment of peak performance. Make sure the words you use are neutral (i.e. not tied to the past or the future). You now have your very own set of mental re-focus cues, and, a strategy to deal with a performance situation where you might veer off into a time-warp. This kind of strategy is "task-relevant," meaning; it is directly related to achieving peak performance.

Ultimately, and with consistent practice, the goal is to reach a state where you can even let go of the mental re-focus strategy itself; allowing the body's natural intelligence to take over. At this point, we return to Takuan Soho's notion of "no-mind," which I talked about earlier. With practice, you begin to discover that you can actually think with your whole body (rather than just in your head). You learn to trust your body's natural intelligence to do what it needs to do in the moment. Initially, the challenge is to embody your re-focus cues, so that you can remind yourself to come back to the present moment. Remembering a re-focus strategy, calls you back to the present moment, where your thinking mind needs to be, in order to effectively serve your body's intentions. Remembering to be present, means to re-establish unity among the "members" of your body (e.g. arms, legs, feet, torso and head). Here's a slogan for martial artists: "Re-membering avoids dismemberment."

In a few simple steps, let's now sum up the main points about thinking-based re-focus strategies:

Step 1: First, you need to have enough somatic self-awareness to know when you slip into a past or future "time warp." This takes practice. One way to gain such practice is to follow the advice outlined in Chapter 7: *Surfing the Edge of Chaos: Mindfulness in the Midst of Action.*

Step 2: When you recognize you are in a time-warp, you learn to gently shift your attention from the past or future, back into the present, by using a re-focus strategy (which can be a one-word cue or a collection of cue words). Here you are learning to park unhelpful thoughts while maintaining present-tense focus.

Step 3: Your thinking mind will inevitably wander again (that's what normal minds do—but I'm aiming to get you on the road to developing an *extra-ordinary* mind). Be gentle with it. Repeat steps 1 and 2.

Step 4: Over time, you will be able to let go of the thinking-based re-focus strategy, and be able to bring yourself back to the present without thought. In essence, you begin, to "think with your whole body."

Anchors

A ship has an anchor to prevent it drifting away due to wind or current. In the same vein, the technique I will explain here is a way to keep you "anchored" to the present moment. It will protect you from the winds and currents of your thoughts, which can easily take you away from your immediate experience. Anchoring, then, is a technique for getting you back into the present moment, so you can respond with clarity and focus, to what is unfolding right in front of you.

Unlike the thinking-based re-focus strategies described earlier, anchors are physical in nature. Where previously you were asked to use your very own "thinking mind" (a verbal cue) to get you back to the present, you are now going to use a physical gesture first, to achieve the same result. Not only do physical anchors (some small gesture you do with your body) aid in getting you back to the present, they can also have additional positive side effects. For example, researchers Schubert and Koole discovered that a person's self-esteem was heightened by the simple act of making a fist.[7] We will tackle this in depth later, in Principle 3 "Body Attitude Matters."

The purpose of anchoring is to connect a physical movement that you can do during a performance event, to re-center yourself back in the present moment. Unlike re-focus cues that are cognitive (something you think about in your mind), anchoring is *somatic* in nature (meaning it activates your body's innate intelligence and memory). Anchoring, involves using a physical gesture, such as clenching a fist, to remind you to reconnect with your body's felt sense.

I have found, that anchoring is a great tool to use whenever it is hard to let go of past- or future-thinking. I have used anchors successfully in conjunction with cognitive re-focus strategies, too. As a combination, they can amplify each other.

---

[7] Shubert, T.W., and Koole, S. L. (2009). "The Embodied Self: Making a fist enhances men's power-related self-conceptions." *Journal of Experimental Social Psychology.*

For example, if I find myself moving into a "time-warp" while sparring, just squeezing my fist hard inside my glove brings me back to the present. This then allows me to immediately switch over to my cognitive cue words, to help me re-focus further. At times—and with practice, of course—just squeezing a fist inside my glove is enough to let go of those past/future thoughts. I don't even have to use my re-focus cue words.

As with cue words, anchoring can only be effective, if you are aware that you are off task in the first place. As soon as you become aware of a cognitive time-warp, immediately use a previously chosen anchoring technique to bring yourself back to the present moment, and then, if needed, switch over to a re-focus cue word, as mentioned earlier.

Many types of gestures can work as anchoring techniques—some work better for some people than they do for others. When working with my son on the soccer field, for instance, we found that if he got stuck in past/future thinking about his performance, making a fist, holding it above his head, and then visualizing he was "flushing" those thoughts away, worked exceptionally well for him. You need to find an anchoring technique that works best for you. Just remember: It needs to be a *physical* action. It doesn't have to be some big and obvious gesture that everyone can see. Instead, it can be a small, subtle anchor like my son's, something most people wouldn't even notice. And no, punching your boss in the face is not an anchoring technique. Sorry!

Anchoring can take place during a performance event, during a break while you wait to go back in to a stressful meeting, or just before you step on stage to give a speech. It is important to emphasize though, that you should use anchoring sparingly. For example, if you find that tapping your gloves together gets you back into the present after you make a mistake while sparring, you don't want to constantly tap your gloves together every single time you make an error, or if you feel that the sparring game is just not working out. If you overdo your anchors, your opponent is likely to pick up on this and will be able to use this knowledge against you. An observed anchor is like a flashing signal: "I'm vulnerable, and need to regain my balance." That's why, especially in business, it's important to develop anchors for yourself that are not obvious, that cannot be picked up on easily. Remember, though, that a lot of communication is non-verbal. A "Sleight-of-hand" approach to your anchoring techniques is important in order to keep a tactical advantage.

In-Between Performance Re-Focus Strategies

Interestingly, the biggest mental game mistakes I have seen, both in competitive sparring and in business, happen during the breaks.

For instance, between rounds, fighters often go sit down, or talk about their performance with someone else, until the bell rings for the next round. In many such cases, the fighter either spends the entire time running over what he did wrong in the previous round, dissecting his performance, or trying to plan what to do next. This often includes *predictive avoidance strategies*—where certain strategies that were unsuccessful in a previous round are rejected by the fighter, who now convinces himself not to use these strategies in future rounds.

Much of the time between rounds is spent on future expectations, or fusing to past mistakes. As a consequence, fighters go into the next round unfocused and apprehensive, because they are unsure of what approach to take next. Even worse, they end up trying to force things to work, just because that is what they had planned previously.

Unfortunately, as many of us who have competed or sparred on a regular basis know, the outcome of being unfocused is often disastrous, and can lead to choking.

As with the other re-focus strategies already discussed, the goal here is to keep oneself focused in the present moment, and nowhere is this more important than *between rounds* or in a *break*. That's why I teach clients to develop the habit of In-Between Performance Re-Focus Strategies (IPRS).

IPRS should be a "routine," a planned action. As in all re-focus strategies, it is something you need to have already developed, worked on, and rehearsed previously. An IPRS routine can be cognitive in nature, but I have found that a physical, embodied action works best. While you could combine both a physical action with a cognitive one, I suggest you don't develop a purely cognitive IPRS routine. Almost always, embodied action is most effective.

For example, when you come off the mat after a sparring round where a lot of thinking was going on (even if you were using mental re-focus or anchoring strategies), it is natural to reflect on your performance. After all, that's what breaks are for: To give you time to rest and recuperate a little, to think back over what just happened, evaluate yourself, and plan out your next moves, right? *Wrong!* While, yes, you can use breaks to rest a little, let go of tension, and get your breath back, breaks between rounds are *not* the time to "get into your head" and start analyzing what worked and what didn't. The more you do this, the more anxious you become for the next round or, in business, the next stage of the meeting.

Use your breaks, to *give your mind a break*. Let your body relax a little, and when it does, your natural embodied intelligence will automatically guide you the moment you step back into the fray. Of course, by now it won't be a surprise to learn that one of the best ways to let your body relax is to focus your awareness right in the present moment. And one of the best ways to achieve that is through *anchoring*.

The more you think about what you should be doing, the more you tighten up, not just physically, but mentally, too. This is why an IPRS routine keeps your body in the action (keeping the body's engine running), but equally serves as a way to ground you back in the present. If there is one overriding reason to have an IPRS routine, it is, to allow you to let go of what just happened.

My sparring partners hate my in-between IPRS round routine. Anyone who has sparred with me enough knows that when I center myself between rounds, getting really focused, you can bet a million dollars that I come back into the next round stronger. My sparring partners aptly named it Rodney's "Circling Shark" routine. Here's what it looks like: Coming off the mat, I ceremonially shake off the round that just ended. Essentially, I am shaking the mistakes away: I literally shake my hands next to my side. I then spend the entire time before the next round walking in a circle around the mat. At times, I circle in only one direction when not too tired; but, when I am really fatigued, I circle three times to the left, change direction, and then circle three times to the right. While all of this is happening, I am focused on my out-breath (discussed in Principle 5). As in other re-focus strategies, this IPRS routine is neutral. I am not thinking about what went wrong in the last round; and I am not planning what to do next when the new round begins. My goal is simply to get myself back to the present moment.

Most importantly, my IPRS routine keeps me in the game by moving my body, and keeping it ready for action, yet at the same time, ensuring that my focus is on being present. Your IPRS is something you do in-between a performance event. In sparring it happens between rounds; in tough negotiations it happens in the breaks. It's a routine; so in that sense it needs to be a pattern, a sequence that is observed time and time again. Part of all this training, IPRS included, is to create *rituals* for the body, so that your body-mind can immediately recognize the message: "Now is the time to get grounded and centered."

Everything I have covered so far, is about training your mind-body to keep present (or to regain being present) during a performance, when you face a stiff challenge—whether in sports or in the corporate world. These re-focus rituals teach your mind-body to stay away from past/future thinking, which otherwise would make effective performance difficult at best. The more I practice these re-focus strategies, the quicker I am able to access them. In my case, I have practiced these routines over and over to the point where, for me, they are now automatic.

Pre-Performance Routine

Peak performance is not just about staying focused in the midst of action. Performing at your peak also means you need to get ready for action. You need to be prepared. Enter, "*pre-performance* routines." Similar to an IPRS routine, a pre-performance routine is something you want to do before you even enter a performance venue. The purpose of the pre-performance routine is, (yes, you guessed it), to help you become present for the upcoming event.

My friend, John Michael Morgan, author of *Brand Against The Machine*, travels the world giving presentations. Getting on stage, in front of a large audience, can be daunting. Planning what you are going to say, rehearsing what may or may not go right, etc. can get you so worked up before an event, that you end up "choking" (affecting your ability to speak or act clearly and coherently). John found a way to overcome this by simply stretching just before a speaking event. It helps him get his body loose so he feels comfortable. Then he prays and asks God to help him say something that will impact someone's life; he then follows this by listening to rock music, because that gets his energy going. Finally, just at the point before he is ready to run on to the stage, he says one more quick prayer, and then it's go-time. That's John's pre-performance routine, and he does it every single time that he has to give a talk. Again, you need to develop your own routines to help you loosen up and get present. Each of us just needs to find out what works best for *ourselves.*

Another important aspect of having a pre-performance routine is to enable you to let go of the busyness, and buzz, of your day. Clients often come to me straight from work, throw on gloves, and want to go straight into sparring. I don't recommend this. More often than not, they are still holding on to what went wrong during the day, or they are focusing on how stressed or fatigued they feel; or, they might even be second-guessing themselves as to why they would put themselves through this experience to begin with. Yep, believe it or not, people pay me to hit them.

Remember: Holding onto the past, or having future expectations before or during a performance, often causes distress, and, as a result, your performance can fall apart. A pre-performance routine not only motivates you for the upcoming event; it is also the first step to becoming present for the event ahead.

A pre-performance routine can start as early as the car ride over to the gym or the business meeting. For example, I encourage my clients to create a music playlist that inspires and motivates them to train—like John listening to rock music as part of his pre-performance routine.

Once in the gym, even wrapping your hands in a specific sequence (e.g. starting with the left hand first, then the right), then doing the same when putting on your gloves, and finally inserting a mouthguard . . . are "rituals" that can act as an effective pre-performance routine. When I travel around the world to coach, I get up early, work a series of breathing routines, listen to my seminar music playlist, and I am ready to go. I do this in my hotel room, prior to getting on that stage. And it works.

In each case, the goal is for you to ground yourself in the present moment, to let go of irrelevant thoughts, stop planning or building expectations for what might lie ahead; and instead, do what you can to be centered. This prepares you for the performance and whatever experiences are about to unfold.

This pre-performance period should be spent building embodied trust, allowing the body's natural intelligence to make the right decisions during performance. You should never plan or strategize for a meeting (martial or business) or a speech, just moments before the event—and certainly not during the live event itself. Preparation should happen during *training;* not during a performance.

Principle 3

Body Attitude Matters

How you hold your body not only changes your physiology, it also changes how you think and feel. In the previous chapter, I dealt mainly with the thinking mind, and how to get it on track in the present. I also highlighted the importance of coming up with an anchoring technique. This should have given you the first clue as to the power that the body has, to not only change the way you think, but also how you feel.

My experience has shown that a person's thinking mind is expressed in body movement and posture. This, in turn, can positively or negatively affect a person's physical movement. On the other hand, each person's physical movement can also affect his or her thinking mind. It's a two-way street, a never-ending mind-body feedback loop. The mind-body feedback loop can be positively or negatively affected depending on your mental attitude, and equally the quality of your movement and posture.

But, what does this mean?

For a very long time, people have held a widespread misconception that mind and body are separate—as if mind and body exist in entirely different universes. This isn't the case at all. As we will see, although mind and body are *inseparable*—they always form a unified whole—they are nevertheless *distinct.* In other words, mind does not *equal* body or brain. All bodies and their parts are *physical objects;* minds are *non-physical subjects.* In short, minds feel and think about what the body does. Mind and body, therefore, are *different* but *inseparable.*

As noted earlier, the mind-body split began back in the seventeenth century when the famous French philosopher René Descartes, declared not only that mind and body were different, but also, *separate.* He defined any body (i.e. anything made of matter) as extended in space; but, he said, that the mind has no extension in space. Matter or body, then, is "extended stuff," while mind is "thinking stuff" or "feeling stuff." The mind, in other words, is what thinks and feels. This distinction is important, and makes a lot of sense. However, Descartes didn't just make a distinction between mind and body; he said they were also separate—existing in different domains of reality. He split them apart. And that's when the problems set in.

Descartes' mind-body split made a big impact in Western philosophy, modern science, and society in general. For example, science focuses exclusively on gaining knowledge about the physical world, the world of matter (bodies extended in space). It completely ignores the non-physical domain of mind and consciousness. In fact, science goes even further, and claims that the only reality is physical stuff—matter or energy. Mind, then, is assumed to be some kind of "by-product" from complex interactions between brain cells.

As a result, most people tend to just focus on the physical side of their own lives, believing that what happens in their minds is not all that significant, or even real to their experience. For instance, when I started learning boxing and martial arts, I was told that success depended on nothing more than building up physical strength and skills. While I heard murmurs of something called the mental side of the game, to be honest, it was mostly ignored, or, if acknowledged, no one seemed to have a clue how to train it.

Even today, many martial artists, along with many people in business, ignore the crucial role that mind (including attitude, focus, attention, feeling, and thought) plays in perfecting performance. Thankfully, this is now changing. In a small way, I hope this book contributes to this change.

More and more people are realizing that the mind-body split was artificial to begin with. It never really existed (except in the ideas of philosophers and scientists). Others, such as artists, dancers, and master martial artists, have always known that mind and body are like the two sides of a coin—inseparable, but different. They always work together, enhancing each other. And when they work against each other, the result is poor performance.

That's why it is important to recognize the intimate connection between mind and body. Yes, they are obviously distinct and different: Mind is that part of us that thinks, and feels, and chooses. It does not exist in space. It is non-physical. Matter or body, on the other hand, is our "bulk," the part of us that is physical, and takes up space.

Because most people seem to miss this important point, I'll repeat it again, with emphasis: *Even though mind and body are distinct, they are never separate.* As philosopher Christian de Quincey puts it: "Unity does not equal identity." Think of the two sides of a coin: Heads and tails are different, but you can't separate them—they are distinct but unified. That's how it is with mind and body. They are different, but always go together. And that's why it is important for anyone seeking peak performance—from martial artists, to corporate executives—to focus on developing a keener sense of their own mind-body unity; to understand and experience, how what goes on in the thinking mind, affects how the body performs, and likewise what goes on in the body affects the thinking mind. Once you get this, you begin to realize that your mind is not just something sealed up in your skull; it permeates your entire body, all of you—all the way to the tips of your finger and toes.

In sparring, if you face an opponent who is striking at you, it clearly makes sense to make a distinction between your mind and your body. After all, if you get hit, it's your body that can get bruised; but, crucially, your opponent can't actually grab your mind. Your mind doesn't get bruised, at least not physically. The Buddha was right on the money, when he noted: It's not what happens to us on the outside that is the problem; rather, it is how we interpret it on the inside. Getting your inner game right on the inside, then, can make all the difference between winning and losing. You may be bruised up on the outside, but your mind decides if you will give up or not.

Even though body and mind are intimately connected, we know that the mind and body have very different kinds of existence. To repeat: One is non-physical (mind) and the other is physical (body). It follows, then, that we need to develop and master different processes, and different practices for training the body, and training the mind. Working out on the mat, or performing at work, you are engaging in the outer game—which, of course, is important. However, you also need to learn when, and how, to shift to the inner game, where a different set of practices is needed, to develop inner confidence, attention, focus, attitude, and, a present mind.

To sum up: Just because mind and body are distinct, does not mean that they are ever separate; they are embodied in a seamless unity. They always go together: So, whatever is going on in the body, is going to have some impact on what's going on in your mind, your consciousness. And the reverse is true: Whatever is going on in your mind, whatever you are thinking, whatever your attitudes are, whatever your belief systems are, those will have an impact on how your body performs.

People often don't realise that the way they are thinking affects their body movement, and vice versa. How you bring body attitude to the mat—the way you hold your body—will also, in turn, affect your thinking mind. Mind and body work together, influencing each other in this feedback loop.

A growing body of science supports the idea that simple physical gestures can impact your mental attitude. For example, a study by Brion, Petty and Wagner[8] published in the *European Journal of Social Psychology,* examined the ways posture influences our self-confidence. Job applicants were asked to fill out a mock application, which asked them to list their strengths and weaknesses pertinent to the job. One group was instructed to sit up straight as they filled the application, and then asked to rate themselves. A second group was asked to sit slumped over and complete the same application. The applicants who were slumped over had lower self-confidence, as expressed by their answers, than those who sat up straight. This research shows that whether you sit up straight at your desk or slump in your chair impacts the chemicals produced in your brain, which, in turn, affect what goes on in your mind.

A study conducted in 2009[9], by researchers at the University of Illinois at Urbana-Champaign, asked two groups of people to solve a problem that required a solution involving swinging strings. The first group was asked to swing their arms while coming up with a solution, whilst the other group was asked to sit

---

[8] Brion, P., Petty, R.E. and Wagner, B. (2009) "Body posture effects on self-evaluation: A self-validation approach." *European Journal of Social Psychology*, 39, 1053-1064.

[9] Lleras, Alejandro and Thomas, Laura. (2009) "Swinging Into Thought: Directed Movement Guides Insight" in Problem Solving. *Psychonomic Bulletin and Review.*

still and solve the problem. Those who moved solved the problem faster, which demonstrated to the researchers, that our brains can take cues from our bodies to help understand and solve complex problems. This important study changed the way that people think about the impact of the body on the mind, instead of the classical view of the mind only impacting the body.

How your body affects your mind, was further illustrated in a recent study by Carney and Yap of Columbia University, and Cuddy at Harvard University.[10] The study tested the theory that humans, and other animals (like the peacock, for example), express power through open, expansive postures, and they express powerlessness through closed, contractive postures. The researchers wanted to know, "Is power embodied?" What happens if humans posed in powerful stances? Would posing as "powerful," help a person feel and be more powerful? The results, published in *Psychological Science (Online First)*, showed, that it could. In fact, both women and men posed in high-power, non-verbal displays, experienced increased testosterone, decreased cortisol, and increased feelings of power and tolerance for risk. People posed in low-power poses experienced the exact opposite changes. This 2010 study is significant because it suggests that being embodied extends to our physiology, which in turn, can change how we think and feel about ourselves.

All this research confirms that how you hold your body—your *body attitude*—changes how you think and feel. This is really good news for peak performance.

---

[10] Carney, Dana R., Cuddy, Amy J.C., and Yap, Andy J. Power, "Posing: Brief Nonverbal Displays Affect neuroendocrine Levels and Risk Tolerance." *Psychological Science Online First.* Sept. 21, 2010.

It suggests, that by changing how we hold our bodies, we can dramatically im-prove both the way we think, and feel—especially when negative thoughts threaten to derail us. Bruce Lee knew this, too: "Emotion can be the enemy. If you give in to your emotion, you lose yourself. You must be at one with your emotion, because the body always follows the mind." Following this thinking from Lee, I suggest that when negative emotions are present, simply changing how you hold your body—from a stance of no confidence, lack of presence, or slumping over, to one of strength, formidable presence, and shoulders back—will shift those emotions into a positive direction.

So, back to the re-focus strategies I discussed earlier: Just firing off cue words in your head, without *literally* embodying their meaning, will likely result in a less than desirable outcome. You need to *feel your thinking*, not just think your thoughts. Your thinking needs to express what's going on in your body, or, the reverse, your body needs to literally incorporate your thoughts and intentions. When mind and body are aligned in this way, you can adjust or adapt your mind-body attitude accordingly.

For example, in sparring, telling myself to be "tight," just in my mind—without actually creating what that feels like within my body—will result in a disconnect between what I am saying to myself, and what my body is doing. I started off with the mental, thinking side of performance first, because this is realistically the least difficult aspect of mental game to understand—partly because we are so used to thinking all of the time. Thinking is very familiar to all of us.

However, when it comes to engaging our somatic selves, and trusting our bodies to make the right decisions, we, in modern Western culture, are at a disad-vantage. Our education system is overly focused on training our minds, by developing our thinking/cognitive faculties. If the body is acknowledged at all, this is almost always in the context of sports. Following from the philosophy of Descartes, modern education splits mind from body, and trains them separately. In one way, invoking body attitude enables us to counteract this split, and aim at unifying the mind-body.

For most of our lives we have been taught that to achieve anything of value in life takes rational intelligence. But, while reason is one kind of intelligence, the body possesses another, quite different, kind of intelligence. The research studies mentioned earlier highlight this. As Amy Cuddy notes, "Let your body tell you you're powerful and deserving, and you become more present, enthusiastic and authentically yourself."[11] The research paper mentioned earlier from Cuddy, Carney and Yap, reported, that those lab participants who spent two minutes in a room, alone, doing high-power poses (for example, feet up on the desk with fingers laced behind the head), increased their testosterone levels by about 20 percent, and lowered the stress hormone cortisol by about 25 percent. How you hold your body then changes your physiology and, in doing so, changes how you think.

Bottom line: Body attitude has a definite and clear effect on how the mind responds in particular performance environments.

---

[11] http://www.nytimes.com/2014/09/21/fashion/amy-cuddy-takes-a-stand-TED-talk.html?_r=0

Upping Your 'Mental Game'

Sometimes, people find it difficult to get themselves back to the present moment because there's so much stuff going on in their thinking mind. One way to overcome this is to consciously recreate a more effective body attitude. I teach a crouched or "hunchbacked" fighting stance, which in my mind represents the equivalent to a power pose, but for fighting. The same is true if you are having a hard time being present in a meeting because your thinking mind is running wild; it helps to realize that an unfocused mind can be aided in becoming focused, simply by changing the way you hold your body.

I sometimes use the phrase "mental game" as shorthand to imply all of this—otherwise it gets complicated. However, sometimes when I talk about the "mental game," people think I am talking about only what's in your head. Nothing could be further from the truth. The mental game is first and foremost: An embodied feeling that involves awareness of your body, and the sensations flowing through it, at any moment. It's often an emotive process, and one way to enhance your mental game is to engage your body in a correct attitude for the specific situation you find yourself in—be that in a sparring match, or in an office meeting. Simply correcting your body posture is often all you need in the moment to switch your mind from a negative to a positive attitude. In other words, the "mental game" is as much about what is happening in your body, as it is about what is happening in your head. It's very important to make that distinction.

Posturing: Not the Same as Body Attitude

Body attitude certainly has pluses and minuses, and it would be irresponsible not to highlight the negative side here. Some people, what I call the "watermelon boys"—you know the guys who strut around looking like they are carrying imaginary watermelons under their arms, and wearing a T-shirt five sizes too small for them—use posturing to intimidate other people. As we all know instinctively, they do this only to hide deep insecurities inside themselves. While this might be an effective "body attitude" for intimidating other people, and could even come across as tough, it is not the kind of body attitude I'm talking about. I don't want to you to pretend you are in a *National Geographic* special, standing up on hind legs like a grizzly bear, waiving your paws around to chase out intruders.

Posturing is likely as old as fighting (most animals species do it), and can be a powerful ally when needed. And even though the studies mentioned earlier use the term "powerful," it isn't power that comes from presenting a tough-guy or woman attitude. As we well know, such posturing can be used as a bullying tactics in the workplace. Body attitude, first and foremost, is not about threatening your opponent, or co-worker, it's about *you*—about how *you* feel inside. By changing the way you hold your body, you will feel more present; and when you feel more present, you will feel more confident. Confidence is the key to achieving success in anything, especially in tough negotiations. The power of body attitude to produce inner self-confidence, results from the fact that our body and mind are intimately related. While minds and bodies are different, they always go together. That is why it is crucial for professionals to develop a keener sense of what I call their "mind-body interface."

To be poised for real success, we must understand, and experience, how what goes on in our minds, impacts what goes on with our bodies, and vice versa.

The way you hold your body—the body attitude you display—will not only change how you feel about yourself, but also how others perceive you. Better yet, it tells your mind that you are confident.

Principle 4

Surf the Edge of Chaos

"The best way to capture moments is to pay attention. This is how we cultivate mindfulness. Mindfulness means being awake. It means knowing what you are doing."

—*Jon Kabat-Zinn,* Wherever You Go, There You Are

As a martial artist, mindfulness has been an integral part of my training and coaching for many years—way before it became popular. My first introduction to mindfulness was more than two decades ago, when I first went to Thailand to train in Muay Thai. Most of the fighters at the Muay Thai camp I attended were Buddhists too, and going to the temple to meditate was a regular occurrence. It took me a long time to figure out why mindfulness is so important, especially when it comes to peak embodied performance. Today, mindfulness is everywhere, and seems to be the panacea for all kinds of ills, from helping with stress, pain, or just to be happier.

What *Is* Mindfulness?

Mindfulness can be described as awareness of the here and now, experienced with openness, interest, and receptiveness. The qualities of mindfulness are embodied through contact with the observing self (the witness) and expansiveness (curiosity and non-judgment). Mindfulness teacher Jon Kabat-Zinn defined mindfulness as: "Paying attention, on purpose, in the present moment, as if your life depended on it, non-judgmentally." Naturally, I like the phrase, "as if your life depended on it"—because it literally can, especially for those of us engaged in *full-contact living*

"As if your life depended on it" is an apt metaphor, and, as I just implied, it could be more than a metaphor in some situations. At one extreme, martial arts are intended as a primer for self-preservation, where actions that could result in life or death may be a reality. In a more realistic sense, during training, sparring experiences can bring up intense emotional and mental responses, where second-guessing oneself could lead to injury, or often, just as painfully, a wounded ego.

Approaching sparring, then, "as if your life depended on it" means completely immersing yourself in the experience, and paying full attention to what is happening in the present moment. Effective mindfulness practice requires, that you don't judge your performance as it unfolds. In its purest form, it means surrendering to what is. Surrendering in this way is not new in the warrior mindset.

Samurai warrior, Takenaka Shigeharu said: "One finds life through conquering the fear of death within one's mind. Empty the mind of all forms of attachment, make a go-for-broke charge and conquer the opponent with one decisive slash." He knew all too well that attachment to sensations, images, feelings, thoughts (SIFTs) can lead to defeat. We can take Shigekata's notion of "empty the mind of all forms of attachment" as, a mindful approach to approaching the chaos of life or challenges in the ring. To die to the past and the future, in other words not attaching to it, to be fully non-judgmentally present during your sparring experience is to accomplish "conquering the fear of [making mistakes] in one's own mind."

Whereas meditation teachers such as Jon Kabat-Zinn talk of "mindfulness," I extend that idea and practice to the body-mind in action. That's why I call it "mindfulness-in-action." Being mindful-in-action, during performance, allows you to be centered in the present moment. By cultivating mindfulness-in-action, you learn to not judge your thoughts and emotions, and instead, learn to self-regulate by focusing your attention on, and expanding your awareness of, what's happening around you.

In many ways, I share Tony Robbins' sentiments, expressed in an interview with author and entrepreneur Tim Ferriss, that sitting meditation might not be for everyone. In fact, trying to get my executive clients to sit still on a zafu is virtually impossible. Because of this, I started practicing, and teaching, what I termed *mindfulness-in-action*. It turns out that I am not alone in the call for this approach.

Tony Schwartz, CEO and founder of The Energy Project, and bestselling author, writing in the *New York Times,* notes, that what is needed is mindfulness in action, not what a person can do with their eyes closed. Further Deepak Sethi, CEO of Organic Leadership, recognizes the potential application of mindfulness to the work environment, yet notes that the challenge is to be mindful in the crucible of work, not just when sitting quietly in a meditation chair.

What Is Mindfulness-In-Action?

I have always found it difficult to meditate in a candle-lit room, sitting on a zafu, with the calming effect of sandalwood incense wafting in the air. While I can, and do, welcome the peace of mind that comes from being still, the challenge comes when I need to apply mindfulness to rubber-on-the-road real-life pressures. Sitting on a zafu or meditation cushion seems to me somewhat alien to the real world we all have to live and work in. Life isn't a monastery, it's fast-paced, unpredictable, and will Judo throw you if given half a chance.

Nowhere was this more evident, than when a client who is a psychologist, trained in mindful-based cognitive therapy, came to me for training. After a few sessions of teaching him the basics, and discussing being mindful in action (something he fervently claimed he didn't need), I got him to move around and throw some punches at my trainer's mitt, while he also tried to defend some attacks from me. The pace wasn't hard, and there was no way he could get injured, yet he immediately lost all his focus, and fell apart. As he told me later, "I teach this [mindfulness] all the time to my clients, yet today I realized I couldn't do it even under some mild pressure."

I suspect this realization—the difficulty involved in translating sitting mindfulness, into real-life action, where it counts—happens for many people who have plunged into the mindfulness revolution. Taking mindfulness off the zafu, and into the world, turns out to be harder than they thought. (I want to make it clear, however, that I am not suggesting meditation has no benefit; just that in my experience, it is not enough for dealing with physically challenging or threatening situations.) As Tony Schwartz, a long time meditator himself, noted: We need mindfulness in action. The question then is; how do you train for this?

Given my background, my solution has been to use martial arts. I do not mean martial arts in the sense of learning to "fight," but rather, learning to use it as a somatic self-awareness discipline—a tool to help my executive clients embody mindfulness-in-action.

Mindfulness-in-action opens you to somatic self-awareness, making you aware of your automatic behaviors. As you learn a new way to relate to your thoughts and emotions, you will discover that you can choose new behaviors to replace the old ways of dealing with your automatic reactions. This leads to greater functional performance in any life endeavor.

Mindfulness-in-action is designed to develop your ability to notice your internal processes (thoughts/emotions/sensations/feelings) non-judgmentally, and to cultivate the ability to refocus, on purpose, to deal with the task at hand. In this way, at its peak, mindfulness-in-action transcends both re-focus and body attitude strategies.

In essence, then, mindfulness-in-action is a state of being that is completely focused in the present. At the same time, it allows you to more easily and rapidly recognize distractions as they occur (irrelevant cues), and to use mindful embodied attention to refocus (anchoring) on the task at hand (re-focus strategies).

Mindfulness-in-action is not a form of relaxation, nor is it a form of positive thinking. Instead, the main objective of mindfulness is: To promote and enhance somatic self-awareness. In mindfulness, therefore, it is just as important to be aware of your negative mental states, thoughts, and emotions: as it is to notice your positive states. What matters is a deepening of somatic self-awareness. As you develop greater somatic self-awareness, you will discover that mindfulness gives you an enhanced ability to notice, and then to be free from, habitual mental and behavioral reactions.

Mindfulness is a process of embodied reflection. It allows access to bodily-based awareness that exists prior to habitual thought patterns and preconceptions. At the same time, it allows you to witness your mind, and what it is doing. Insights gained through mindful awareness—witnessing the inner flow of mind-body and its reaction to the outer world—provide an opportunity to engage in corrective somatic self-awareness (i.e. using all the tools in this book appropriately).

Mindfulness Is *Not* About Avoidance

Often when one speaks of mindfulness as not judging our inner experiences, and allowing them to be, it seems that what is being asked, is to avoid how we feel and think. Most people fuse to their thoughts and feelings, becoming lost in their story. Mindfulness is never about avoiding experiences you are having now; but rather, it is a way to help you become more aware of your in-the-moment experiences, exactly as they occur. For many people, the insight that is gained is liberating, to know that you are not your thoughts and feelings, and that you can chose how to respond, rather than having your thoughts and feelings respond for you on autopilot.

Benefits of Mindfulness

Bringing mindfulness to your work and life will inevitably have consequences; and according to all the research, as well as what we'd expect from common sense, all the consequences of increased mindfulness are beneficial. It's hard to imagine a situation where being more aware of what is *actually happening* might be detrimental. Mindfulness, after all, is simply intentionally paying attention, without judgment or bias, to whatever is happening in your mind-body and environment *right now.* Doing so "as if your life depended on it," adds a more intense level of motivation and sharpens your focus and clarity. Daphne, Davis, Jeffrey, and Hayes[12] of Pennsylvania State University, did a comprehensive review of evidence-based research into mindfulness, and published the results in a report called *What Are The Benefits Of Mindfulness?* They concluded that sufficient research now confirms that mindfulness is effective in regulating our emotions by altering activity in our brains; it increases our flexibility to respond to challenges, and, offers interpersonal benefits, such as enhanced satisfaction in relationships.

---

[12] Davis, Dr. Daphne M. and Hayes, Dr. Jeffrey A. What are the benefits of mindfulness? A Practice Review of Psychotherapy-Related Research. American Psychological Association Journal, July/August 2012. Vol. 43. No. 7 Print Version: P. 64

A study published in *Social Cognitive and Affective Neuroscience*, authored by D. J. Siegel[13], determined that mindfulness enhances functions associated with the middle prefrontal lobe area of the brain. These key functions included self-insight, morality, intuition, and fear-modulation.

In other words, you are at the peak of your mental game; when you can focus your mind, and remain unconcerned or worried about the future or reacting to what happened in the past. Sound familiar? By now, we could call this the central message and lesson of this book: *Peak performance goes hand-in-glove with a mind sharply focused on the present moment. Full-contact living*—requires training your mind to avoid getting sucked into a "time-warp" that takes your attention into the past, or the future, *whatever the circumstances.* And one of the most effective ways to do this is through mindfulness practice.

While I have only cited a couple of important research findings into mindfulness (there are dozens more), they show that being aware of one's inner state, with curiosity, and without judgment, where we allow whatever to arise, without becoming lost in our story, is powerful in changing our lives.

Applying Mindfulness-In-Action

For most people most of the time, thinking just runs on automatic. To be mindful and play your embodied mental game at your best, you need to break the habit, become intentional in your choices, and know how you to direct your mind in the moment.

---

[13] Siegel, D. J. (2007a) Mindfulness training and neural integration: Differentiation of distinct streams of awareness and the cultivation of well-being. Social Cognitive and Affective Neuroscience, 2, 259-263.

A good starting point is just to sit and simply be aware of whatever arises. You don't have to change anything, there is no need to judge, just *notice*. This is called "engaging your observing self." One of the most amazing features of being human is the ability we all share to reflect on, and observe, the inner workings or our mind-body—our sensations, images, feelings, and thoughts (SIFTs).

However, if you really want to get the most out of being mindful, try doing it in the midst of some chaos. It doesn't have to be a life-or-death kind of chaos; just the kind that gets you riled up, both emotionally and cognitively. Getting stuck in traffic can do that for most people. As Zen master Ta Hui noted: "Zen practice in the midst of activity is a million times superior to that pursued in silence."

The Undisturbed Mind

Yagu Jubei, one of the most famous and romanticized of the samurai warriors in Japan's feudal era, urged us to develop an "undisturbed mind," likening it to the "calm body of water reflecting the brilliance of the moon." Only by emptying the mind of all its monkey-chatter will you realize the undisturbed mind.

In essence, the undisturbed mind perceives sensations, images, feelings, thoughts (SIFTs), and memories exactly as they are, not what they appear to be (or how we would like them to be). An undisturbed mind has the ability to observe whatever your thoughts are telling you, and to notice when they don't match reality. The state of "undisturbed mind," then, involves realizing that the things the mind tells us are, really, just conditioned or learned internal events, and do not always coincide with actual reality. Realizing this, you now have the advantage of seeing, that just because something shows up in your thoughts does not necessarily require action. Cultivating an undisturbed mind, therefore, is a great way to conserve energy and to use it to optimal effect.

Thoughts are not the real event. In other words, our thoughts might seem to us to accurately represent reality (that's why we believe them); however, every thought is always an *abstraction* (a mental snapshot), and, therefore, necessarily distorts reality to some degree. Most of the time, most of us take it for granted that what we think is mostly real. In fact, that's the general definition of sanity. However, when we practice mindfulness, we come to realize that most of our thoughts, most of the time, *do not* match reality. Instead, they are like biased, distorted lenses through which we view the world. Our thoughts are always distorted by our emotional biases, our preferences, and our mental habits.

In other words, with mindfulness we come to see that the "normal" state of mind of most people is tinged with a little (or perhaps a lot) of insanity. Now, that might sound a little extreme. Throughout history, however, the great sages and mystics who report having attainted enlightenment, tell us that, indeed, by comparison, the general condition of human minds is somewhat insane. But because this condition is the norm for just about everyone, we fail to notice the frequent mismatches between our thoughts and reality. We get lost in our ego-obsessed stories, and we hardly ever know it. It usually takes a crisis to wake us up, to notice how out-of-touch with reality we have been. In fact, that's what "enlightenment" means: *Waking up to what is.* To live mindfully "as if your life depended on it", then, is a precondition for *full-contact living*.

Think about it (no pun intended): When you have a thought about something (e.g. your opponent, or your own performance), you probably tend to believe that's the way it "really is." But a thought is always just some abstraction in your head, and may have little, or indeed nothing, to do with what is actually going on. Your thought is just that—a *thought*. Meanwhile, reality is right there in your face, and doesn't give a damn about what you happen to think. Native American warrior-poet-musician, John Trudell said it well in one of his songs: "I slammed into reality, and reality didn't even blink."

For instance, few people I work with would avoid the thought, "sparring is fun," but all will try to avoid the thought, "I might fail in sparring." Both are just thoughts. Many people try to avoid the latter—for example, by not showing up for training that day. In this instance, that person has "fused" with his or her thoughts, and the thoughts have become reality for them.

Thoughts in sparring, life, or the boardroom can be triggered by a wide variety of stimuli (visual, auditory, etc.), that are, in turn, associated with historical or biographical events in your past. Cultivating mindfulness-in-action, and achieving an undisturbed mind, enables you to recognize that your thoughts are a silent, self-spoken language you have learned throughout your life. They are often associated with particular biographical events, and can trigger cascades of other compelling thoughts about "who I am," "how others see me," "what's going to happen," and "what just happened" . . . we get sucked into our stories. Mindfulness reveals all this to us as we observe how our thoughts naturally come and go. Usually they come wrapped in some kind of super "mental-velcro," hooking us into the drama of our self-created stories. In mindfulness, however, we can learn to let them come, and then let them go, just as readily. That way, they lose their mental "stickiness" and don't hook us in. But it's up to us to allow our thoughts to naturally come and go, just like the rising and falling of our chest as we breathe. An undisturbed mind has the ability to simply observe this arising and disappearing of our thoughts, and to choose where to direct attention.

Without a doubt, thoughts have meaning—accumulated during your life-long learning process. However, let me be clear about something at this point: I am not suggesting you try to avoid having thoughts, or to suppress them when they arise, as they inevitably will. That will just backfire and undermine your ability to stay present. In fact, the more you try to control your thoughts, the more you will disturb your mind.

And, this is probably as good a time as any to point out another widespread misconception about mindfulness, or meditation in general: Many people think that meditation is about stopping your thoughts. It's not. Meditation is simply letting your mind do what it naturally does, and *observing* it as it does so—without judgment or interference. That's it. You can expect plenty of thoughts, emotions, feelings, and god-knows-what-else, to arise in your mind-body as you mediate or practice mindfulness. Your "job," as a mindfulness warrior, is to simply *observe* whatever happens, and *let it be.*

The key point to get here is that even though thoughts are natural and inevitable, it's *not* inevitable that we believe our thoughts, to mistake them for what is really real. That's where we can exercise the power of choice: To recognize and acknowledge that our thoughts might well be, and most likely are, out of step with reality. But, as always, to do so *without judgment* or self-recrimination. No sense beating yourself up because you're human, and have a human mind dominated by an ego that convinces you that your thoughts equal reality. That's natural. Instead of blaming yourself for having thoughts you don't want and getting disconnected from reality, just let them come and go as they automatically will. You don't have to do anything with them—not believe them, not try to stop or suppress them, not try to change them, not get sucked into them . . . Just *let them be.*

Meditating with a mind undisturbed happens when you learn the difference between not trying to avoid or suppress your thoughts, and just simply letting them come and go. My friend philosopher Christian de Quincey has expressed it this way: "You can't help having beliefs, but you don't have to *believe* your beliefs." He points out that we have little or no choice about having thoughts or beliefs (it's what our minds evolved to do); but, we do have a choice about whether or not we believe our beliefs to be true. We don't have to fall into the blindness of believing that our thoughts and beliefs reflect reality. The thing about every belief is that it can be more or less right or wrong.

Instead of believing our beliefs, then, de Quincey suggests that we would do better to cultivate what he calls "experience beyond belief." He means what I have been saying in different ways throughout this book: *Pay attention to your embodied sensations or experiences, for that's your key to accessing what's really happening right now.*

Reality always happens *now,* in the present moment; and that's precisely when experience happens—*right now,* in the present moment. Therefore, it follows that the best way to know what's really happening, is to become more aware of what we are actually experiencing, and not get lost in our abstract thoughts and distorted beliefs. As de Quincey frequently says: We need to learn to *feel our thinking* (an embodied process), rather than merely thinking our thoughts (a disembodied mental process). Instead of thinking about our thoughts (which is what we do most of the time), we can train ourselves to *experience our thinking,* to notice how our thoughts arise, and trigger associations, spinning us off into the never-ending story that has become the backdrop, and soundtrack, to our life.

Developing an undisturbed mind, then, is a way to alter the context within which your thoughts are experienced. This empowers you to detach from your thoughts that otherwise are likely to undermine or sabotage you. Many of our thoughts connect together as a coherent narrative, and follow a more or less rational process. However, below the surface, in our unconscious, our thinking mind is almost always also hooked into our emotions, and this ends to blur the edges of logic and reason. An undisturbed mind, achieved through mindfulness, gives us the "mental distance" to notice how our emotions color our thoughts, and that our thoughts are always just that—*thoughts* and nothing more.

In mindfulness, you view your thoughts and emotions as neither good nor bad. Nevertheless, mindfulness-in-action involves learning to ask yourself: "Are my thoughts helpful to achieving the task at hand?" Notice it's not the fact that you are having thoughts that matters (you will have them come what may); it's whether your thoughts are relevant to the immediate situation you face.

As you practice mindfulness, either sitting, or better still, in action, you will come to see the distinction between you, the *person,* and your thoughts. You realize that you have your thoughts, they don't have you. You are not the object; you are the *subject* thinking about the object.

Let's now quickly look at some ways to know when you are operating from an undisturbed mind or a fused mind—one stuck to thoughts and emotions.

Often when you are fused to your thoughts, you don't want to talk about the experience you just had. You might, for instance, tell people that talking about them is too difficult or frustrating. Internally, you just wish they would go away.

Along with this you feel an emotional tightness in your chest. Conversely, when your mind is undisturbed your thoughts are diffused. You are able to laugh at yourself when you make mistakes. Even though initially you may begin to think about right and wrong, catching yourself in the story you are creating you are able to abandon that story midstream. Then, when talking about your thinking, you can reflect on it as a separate entity: "There goes my mind again, telling me I am messing up in sparring," or "in a meeting." Even though you might be confused about the thoughts you are having, you are fine with that. You accept that your mind's ego is a judgmental SOB, and that it does its work automatically. You don't judge your mind for judging you—for that way, lies the road to ruin. You just *let it be.* You have your thoughts, they don't have you. "If my thoughts are not real, what do I do with them?" This thought has probably crossed your mind. And that's where mindfulness leads to mindfulness-in-action.

The Observing Self

Mindfulness, when practiced diligently, can be a gateway to accessing a transcendent sense of self. What does this mean? Well, without going into a lot of detail, it refers to a state, or quality, of consciousness, that transcends our usual day-to-day mind, that is dominated by our ego. The ego, in case you were wondering, is the part of your mind that you call "I." Your ego is your sense of individual personal identity. When used well, the ego helps us take care of our bodies by navigating and guiding us through life. However, besides its usefulness, the ego can also be a block to self-development and optimal performance in life.

Like our thoughts (which, by the way, are produced by the ego), the problem is not having an ego, it's when we let our egos *have us*—when we let our egos take control. The best way to keep your ego in check is to cultivate a sense of a deeper transcendental self. This is your natural background state of consciousness, compared to which your ego is just a tiny spec.

It's called "transcendental" because it goes beyond the small ego-self, that most of us think is the essence of who we are. By cultivating a sense of transcendental self, you can dissolve the illusions that keep you trapped in your ego. You experience an expansive consciousness that seems to be infinite. One of the most common characteristics of transcendental consciousness is that it is always present and unchanging.

Another term for the transcendental self is the "Observing Self"—the part of us we recognize as the person behind the experiences that flow through our lives. However, as the name indicates, the Observing Self is not the experiences themselves; rather, it is the "Witness" who notices or observes our experiences.

The Observing Self, then, is contrasted with the self-as-content, which is the conceptual self most people identify with. The conceptual self (your ego) is made up of your self-evaluations, judgments, and categorizations. In others words, it is how you define yourself to other people ("I am kind,""I am strong," "I am focused," etc.). People generally develop a protective attachment to their conceptual self, their story. And this is where problems arise: People will work very hard to protect their story, even when it is detrimental to their health, family, and relationship with others. The problem is that the human mind is conditioned to identify with its "story"—you know, the incessant, silent, internal narrative we all have going on all the time about who we are, what has happened to us, and why we are miserable or magnificent. It's all just a story. But we think it is who we are. It's not. Identifying with one's story is what I mean by a "fused mind."

An undisturbed mind, on the other hand, is the ability to not identify with your story, with your thoughts, or emotions. It is the ability to recognize or observe the difference between having thoughts, beliefs, or stories, and being identified with those thoughts, beliefs, and stories. You are not your thoughts, beliefs, or stories. You have them, but they do not define you. At your core, you are much more than the products of your ego-mind.

Unfortunately, people tend to use past events as a way to keep their story accurate by not performing at their best now, in other words excuses. In short, our "self-stories" often turn out to be self-fulfilling prophecies. For example, if someone feels that he or she has been timid their whole life, reinforced by a parent they blame, they might ensure that they stay that way by keeping their behavior consistent with their story. They might claim, for instance, that they cannot engage at a higher level of performance in life because of what has happened to them in the past. This becomes a reinforcing nightmare, and the true impetus to change is blocked by this concept of self.

To truly perform at your best at anything, you need to loosen the attachment you have to your conceptual self-your story. By engaging the Observing Self, or what could be thought of as pure self-awareness, you can simply notice each experience as it is—without blame or judgment.

In other words, you can create a psychological stance where you see your thoughts and experiences as "just happening," without threatening your sense of self. A thought or an emotion is not a threat to your sense of self because; "I/here/now" is not defined by your sensations, images, feelings, and thoughts. What defines and limits it, is the story you assign to it. As the Buddha rightly noted, whatever you *think,* you *become.* The inner turmoil we all experience from time to time (yes, it's a natural part of the human condition), arises from our attachment to our ego-stories. Being able to observe what arises in your mind, without judgment, allows you to notice your sensations, images, feelings, and thoughts for what they are—impermanent blips that come and go through your mind, like leaves blowing in the wind. The aim of the Observing Self is to shift your consciousness from being focused on the *content* of your mind, to experiencing consciousness as the *context* of everything that ever happens to you. You want to learn to shift awareness from *self-as-content* to *self-as-context*.

You know you are tied to self-as-content, when you won't make the next move in your life, or in the ring, because you are afraid of your past experiences. You don't want to change or take a risk, because you might be unable to remain constant in your current performance (even if it is not really what you want). Hence the saying: "Better the devil you know, than the devil you don't." You reflect on past failed experiences, and even though this is disturbing it holds you back in a tight vice-like grip.

Like almost everyone else, you are attached to your story (how past negative experiences have affected you), and think these experiences need to be changed before you can make any other changes. I have seen every one of these reasons unfold on the mat, holding people back from achieving greatness in their martial arts training. It doesn't end there, unfortunately: If it is happening on the mat, then it's happening in the rest of your life and career.

One of the most destructive of attachments to self-as-content, happens when someone tries to become what he thinks others (peers, coaches, bosses) want him to be, instead of being guided by his (or her) own inner light.

In contrast, when the Observing Self is in play, you feel comfortable in your own skin—something I struggled with as a child. Growing up where I did, I never felt I could be just be *me*. I had to become, or at least be perceived as being, tough; a no-nonsense, don't-mess-with-me kind of guy. It killed my creative spirit, the person I truly was. Acting from the Observing Self, however, generates a healthy, non-defensive stance toward your experiences. Your private mental events—sensations, images, feelings, and thoughts—no longer define you. You recognize these as travel partners on the journey of life, coming along for the ride, but they don't dictate how you should perform.

From the perspective of Observing Self, you can take a step back and realize that your mind has the ability to create not only helpful and accurate thoughts, stories, mental images, and emotions, but also equally unhelpful and downright crazy ones. When this happens, you can distance yourself from those unhelpful thoughts, personal stories, etc. without being threatened by them. The stories still show up, but they don't suck you in. You can learn to observe them, kind of like watching a movie unfold. When you are able to recognize self-as-context—as the creator of your unhelpful thoughts, feelings, etc.—you can begin to detach, or defuse, from those that stand in the way of you achieving your goals, and, peak performance.

Expansion: Mastery Beyond Expertise

Mindfulness-in-action engages the Observing Self, and usually generates an experience of expansiveness. Expansiveness allows for thoughts, emotions, and sensations to come and go without you struggling with them. It creates "space" for all the contents of your mind to exist simultaneously, without conflict, or without you having to do anything about them. Think of expansiveness as extending your sense of self to include everything about you—all your positive, negative, and neutral attributes. The whole shebang. You "expand" by becoming bigger than any of your thoughts, beliefs, feelings, or emotions, or any combination of these. Your sense of self expands until you become the *context* for all the contents of your mind. You become the "container" of all that you normally think of as "you."

Expansiveness involves accepting your thoughts and feelings exactly as they are—regardless of whether they are pleasant, painful, enjoyable, or frustrating to your performance. Allow yourself to make room for these thoughts and feelings; stop struggling with them and just let them come and go as they naturally do. As my favorite Buddhist teacher Pema Chodron[14], suggests: "The most fundamental aggression to ourselves, the most fundamental harm we can do to ourselves, is to remain ignorant by not having the courage and the respect to look at ourselves honestly and gently."

Mindfulness practice aims to achieve a clear mind, free of thoughts focused on either the past or future. As Zen monk, and teacher, Shunryu Suzuki, noted: "If your mind is empty, it is always ready for anything, it is open to everything. In the beginner's mind there are many possibilities, but in the expert's mind there are few."

In most areas of modern life—from education, to business, to sports, and entertainment—we have been trained to value expertise, and to aim to become an expert in our chosen field. We take it for granted that being an expert is a good

---

[14] Pema Chödrön, *When Things Fall Apart: Heart Advice for Difficult Times*

thing. While *having* expertise is useful, *being* an "expert" has many pitfalls. Here, it's helpful to distinguish between a master and an expert, between *mastery* and *expertise.* Being a master at something is quite different from being an "expert."

Mastery comes from within, and involves cultivating a set of skills, insights, and knowledge that become an effortless part of *who you are* and your self-expression. While mastery, *per se,* is executed effortlessly, the road to mastery requires long hours, of often uncomfortable, even painful, practice. Some researchers believe that to master anything, we need to put in at least ten-thousand hours of practice (see, for example, Malcolm Gladwell's bestseller, *Outliers).*

However, mastery involves more than just clocking up the hours. You also need to keep pushing yourself beyond your present level of achievement, finding the right balance between a challenge that is too easy, and one that is too difficult. Follow the "Goldilocks Rule": Take on challenges that push you just beyond your comfort zone, but not too far. If your challenge is too easy, you won't grow to the next level. If it's too hard, you could be setting yourself up for stress and failure. The "Goldilocks Rule" means: Taking on challenges that are "just right"—not too "hot," not too "cold."

Something else distinguishes mastery from expertise: *Complete mastery is unattainable.* You never "arrive" at full mastery because there is always some room for further growth and improvement. In technical jargon, mastery is "asymptotic"—which means it is always just out of reach; but, we can always move closer and closer to it, without ever getting there. Another major difference: Mastery is a *subjective experience* of effortless competence, skill, and embodied knowledge. Expertise, however, involves developing skills that are *objective,* that others can observe and even measure. Mastery is something you *live;* expertise is something you *demonstrate.*

Furthermore, mastery transcends the "little mind" (the ego), and connects you to something larger and more expansive than your individual sense of "you." In mastery, you step into the *flow* of whatever is happening around you. Your sense of being expands, and you feel your "body" extend out beyond your own skin. Representing yourself as an "expert," by contrast, involves the ego demonstrating its achievements (often to impress others), and fuels the ego's sense of superiority: "I know how to do this, you don't. Watch me. Follow me. I'm the expert." However, when you self-identify as an expert, you risk falling into the trap of thinking you know it all—and that's when you expose yourself to all kinds of risks and dangers. It is much better to let go of any sense of "expertise" that boosts your ego, your "little mind", and, instead, cultivate what Suzuki meant by "beginner's mind."

A master knows that he or she never knows everything there is to know, about any particular activity or area of knowledge. *A true master knows he or she is never a true master!* It is much better to put in the long hours of challenging practice, embody the skills needed for the activity, and then empty your ego-mind of all its "knowledge" or sense of personal achievement. Cultivate a beginner's empty mind, rather than fill your mind with knowledge and expertise. Mastery is not showing off how much you know, or presenting yourself as an expert.

In my experience, engaging life, work, and performance from the Observing Self, with a beginner's mind, opens up more possibilities. It allows for a full, open, undefended psychological contact with any challenges you might face.

This expansive attitude helps you overcome difficult experiences you might encounter in sparring, or in the boardroom—often where all you want to do is to give up, become angry, or make excuses for where you find yourself now. The most difficult aspect of all of this is the idea that: *Regardless of how you are thinking or feeling you can still perform at your best.*

The general view, held by most (including those who teach conventional psychological skills training—PST), is that if one can reduce the impact of, or completely remove, negative thoughts or feelings, this will directly enhance positive performance. In fact, the opposite is true. In the end, the problem is not that thoughts, feelings, or emotions arise (they do this automatically), but rather, how we attach to, or whether we identify with them—the stories we tell ourselves about them. Even a "true" story is still a story, clouded by our opinions, beliefs, personal history, and our environment.

Expansion, then, is a tool you can use to see through the illusions of our self-talk, our stories, it harnesses the power of the beginner's mind. In a state of expansiveness, thoughts and feelings that might seem to get in the way of peak performance, are recognized as just that: Thoughts, or feelings, or stories, and they need not have any impact on the quality of our performance—unless we believe the self-talk. The fact is that thoughts and feelings do not control the outcome of performance—provided you are able to expand and accept them. Adding expansion to the tools outlined in this book, enables you to build real-world confidence.

One thing to be clear about: I am not suggesting that you succumb to your internal states (SIFTs) through *resignation*, by gritting your teeth and putting up with them, or even liking or tolerating them. *Acceptance is not the same as resignation.* The former comes with an empowering sense of "that's just the way it is, and that's okay." Paradoxically, by giving up striving for control, you gain an increased sense of self-agency and responsibility. By contrast, resignation comes with a sense of restriction, of being less-than, a sense of disempowering victimhood.

Expansion is an action-oriented process. It does not mean resigning oneself to an inevitable fate of negative feelings and emotions. On the contrary, you can do something about it. Expansion in this sense, suggests that even though you might think or feel in a way that held you back in the past, making room for these feelings and thinking patterns, and accepting them as a natural occurring process of living, allows you to continue on toward your goals. In short, you can achieve peak performance in spite of your thoughts, fears, and anxieties-and the negative self-talk that these generate.

Expansion, then, means accepting your private experiences, thoughts, feelings, memories, and so on. It is not about passively giving in to your situation in the ring, in life, or the boardroom. It is about taking action, through liberated self-agency, to improve your performance as much as possible. I am not suggesting you should attend to every single thought and feeling that occurs. Instead, I am advocating cultivating expansion, if and when it is needed for peak performance.

In the end, as the great Roman philosopher Marcus Aurelius wrote in *Meditations*: "Perfection of character is this: to live each day as if it were your last, without frenzy, without apathy, without pretense."

Principle 5

Exhale

"Feelings come and go like clouds in a windy sky. Conscious breathing is my anchor."

— *Thích Nhat Hanh,* Stepping into Freedom

While it is important not to confuse your mind with your brain (as many neuro-scientists seem to do), nevertheless, they *are* intimately related. And although your brain does not equal your mind, what happens in one, happens in the other. Someone pricks your finger, or hits you on the head, and this sets off a cascade of events in your nervous system, quickly shooting all the way to your brain. Then you feel the pain. Two kinds of events have just happened: *Physiological* and *Psychological.* The stream of physiological events (pricked or punched) ripples through your body and brain, but the psychological events (feeling pain) happens in your mind. Although they are intimately connected, they are not the same kinds of processes. One is *physical,* the other is *mental.*

Remember, your mind is not a "thing" that exists in space—it is your natural capacity for feeling, awareness, and choice. You will never find a thought, a feeling, a choice, or any other mental content, floating around in space; not because the mind is invisible, but because it doesn't exist as a thing in space. Your mind is what is *aware* of things in space, but it is not itself one of those things. Believe it or not: Your mind is not "inside" your brain, not in the way that your brain sits inside your skull. Mind is the *ability* that brain matter possesses to be aware, to know, and to make choices. But search as you might, you will never find an *ability* located anywhere in anyone's brain, or elsewhere in the body. You might think your thoughts are inside your head, but that's just something you've been conditioned to believe. In other cultures, for instance in ancient Greece, or in some Asian societies, people believed that the mind was located in the heart or the belly.

Your brain, on the other hand, is a lump of immensely complex and wrinkled jelly situated inside your head. This three-pound lump is one of the most intricate pieces of matter in the universe. It controls a great deal of what goes on in your body—including your breathing and heart rate. Without your brain you couldn't think[15]; in fact, you couldn't live. But your brain is not just inside your head. It is, in fact, distributed all over your body through a network of nerves—your nervous system.

I have spoken a lot about the body-mind connection in this book, and I have emphasized the importance of practicing *embodied-mind* for achieving peak performance. For the most part, I have also emphasized in these pages, the importance of cultivating your "mental game," "fluid mind," "empty mind," etc. where I underscore the crucial role of *mind* in creating focus on the present moment. In this chapter, I have also emphasized the important distinction between brain and mind. At this point, however, I want to shift attention to the body side of the body-mind equation, and talk about the importance of what happens in our nervous system.

---

[15] While you need your brain to think; that does not mean thinking happens "in" your brain. Thinking happens in your mind. However, your mind depends on your brain in order to think. Thoughts are highly evolved mental events (worms and amoebas don't think), and thoughts need the machinery of an equally highly evolved, and complex, brain in order to form in the mind. What happens in the brain is reflected in what happens in the mind. While it's not really an accurate metaphor, the following might give you a sense of how what happens in the brain is reflected in the mind. Let's say you are standing in front of a mirror. You see a reflection of your body. Now, while both your body and the mirror are tangible (you can touch them), you cannot actually touch or feel your reflection (it is intangible). Both body and its reflection are real, just like both brain and mind are real. The brain is tangible (a physical object you can touch), but your mind is intangible (you can't touch it). You need the complex organization of matter that is your brain in order for your mind to form the complex organization of mental events we call "thoughts." The key point to remember, though, is this: Even though you need a complex brain to form complex thoughts, your brain does not produce your thoughts and your thoughts are not tucked away somewhere in a corner of your brain. Events in your brain are reflected as events in your mind.

Taking care of your brain and nervous system is really important. But how do you do that? You certainly can't open a hatch in your head to probe or play with your brain (probably just as well!). No, the most effective way to exercise the "muscle" of your brain is through working out with your mind—by developing your mental game. And one of the best ways to do that is by focusing awareness on your breathing.

Have you noticed that, in normal circumstances, you don't have to do anything to take care of your breathing? It just happens naturally, all on its own. Well, that's your brain doing its job behind the scenes. However, sometimes it's useful to take control of your breath, or at least to pay closer attention to it, and, for example, to remember to breathe more deeply and deliberately.

Your breath is one of the most effective links between your mind and your brain, and, therefore, between your mind and your body. Mindfulness of your breathing, then, is a great way to relax your body and become grounded.

In this chapter, I will introduce you to some very basic aspects of your brain—in particular, your autonomic nervous system, or ANS, and its role in balancing your brain, body, and mind.

So now, let's take a quick look at that three-pound piece of intelligent jelly inside your skull, which is connected to all parts of your body through a complex network of nerves.

Your brain sits on top of your spine, which is the main highway for your nervous system, feeding information from your peripheral nervous system (PNS) about what is happening in your body, to your central nervous system (CNS) to be processed in your brain.

Your peripheral nervous system (PNS) has two parts and functions:

External: Your sensory-somatic nervous system, responsible for gathering information about your external environment.

Internal: Your autonomic nervous system (ANS), responsible for monitoring and controlling your internal organs (e.g. heart, lungs, viscera, and glands). Your ANS also affects your motor nerves which determine how your body acts and reacts in response to internal and external stimuli.

Your ANS is mostly beyond conscious control. It operates "behind the scenes," mostly involuntary (by contrast, your sensory-somatic system responds directly to your conscious will).

The ANS, then, perceives your body's internal environment and after information is processed in the Central Nervous System (CNS), the ANS regulates the functions of the internal environment. Most of this is done completely unconsciously.

The ANS has two subdivisions: The parasympathetic and sympathetic nervous systems.

Sympathetic Nervous System: Stimulation of the sympathetic nervous system prepares the body for emergencies. It kicks into action in high stress situations, such as fighting or sparring.

Sometimes referred to as the fight-or-flight system; the sympathetic nerves direct more blood to the muscles and the brain. The heart rate and blood pressure increase, while the blood flow to the digestive and eliminative organs decreases.

Parasympathetic Nervous System: Whereas the sympathetic system gears the body up for action, the parasympathetic system calms it down, bringing your body back into a state of balance.

The parasympathetic balances the sympathetic. Without the parasympathetic nervous system (PNS) for balance, the sympathetic (fight-or-flight) system can overwhelm the body with an over-abundance of energy causing dizziness, confusion, fear, anxiety, or other forms of hyper-arousal and distress.

Breath Enlivens More Than Movement

Whereas most ANS actions are involuntary, some, such as breathing, work in tandem with the conscious mind. This means that breathing is the one tool we can use to have a direct effect on the ANS. Your breathing is the only part of the ANS you can consciously control.

More and more, the medical community is realizing that sympathetic dominance (fear/aggression response) underlies many modern-day maladies, including anxiety and hypertension. While all the variables of the root cause of sympathetic dominance are not completely understood, one root cause is, in fact, suboptimal breathing. Correct breathing brings about autonomic nervous system balance, correcting the state of sympathetic over-activity and parasympathetic under-activity and its consequences-including internal tension, anxiety, and potentially the myriad of other psycho-physiological challenges to health and well being which result from this imbalance.

I am reminded here by the words of Thich Nhat Hanh: "Breath is the bridge which connects life to consciousness, which unites your body to your thoughts." Not only is breath important for calming us down, it is also one of the most important ways to get attention back to the present moment. No matter how much I have trained clients in re-focus strategies, anchors, mindfulness-in-action, or even body attitude, there are times when my mind is racing a thousand miles an hour. In these moments, I can always rely on my breath, specifically my *out-breath*, to tether myself back to the present. I invite my clients to try this simple self-experiment: "Breathe out hard, and try to think." Invariably, they find it's difficult, or nearly impossible, to do. Breathing, then, is your final defense against an unruly mind.

The main point then is to focus on your out breath. The out-breath engages the parasympathetic system. It calms you down, brings your ANS back to homeostasis (balance). If you feeling over-anxious, tense, and hot-tempered, focusing on the out breath is a magic way to calm yourself down. Simply think of your breathing as the waves coming into the shore. The wave that breaks, and rolls back into the ocean is your out-breath. You want it to be smooth and long. Simply allow the in-breath to form itself. The focus should be exclusively on the out-breath, as it is this breathing that activates your parasympathetic nervous system, and as mentioned earlier, this is the part of your ANS that is responsible for calming you down.

When things are kicking off at work, and you feel yourself becoming all worked up, with thoughts racing through your mind, and emotions on the rise, find a place where you can be alone. Spend some time just slowly, and gently, focusing on your out-breath. You will be amazed at the result. When all else fails, breath is, and will always be, my last line of defense in remaining present. Try it!

Principle 6

Roll with the Punches

The mark of a true performer is the ability to rebound from setbacks. Every day, I listen to people talking about what they need to do in order to become successful. A year or more later, I meet the same people, who find themselves in the same place they were years earlier. Clearly, there seems to be a disconnect between what people "want" (or *say* they want), and what people need to do to make it happen. More interesting, many of these people don't even have the convenient excuse of not having access to the people, tools, or processes needed to become successful.

So what's going on? Is it laziness? Perhaps, to a degree . . .

But in my experience people want the success, without the hustle, as Gary Vaynerchuk would say. Sadly, there is no fast-food, drive through version of success. Goals are meaningless, unless you act on them.

While it is important to have a goal, an end destination, success happens in every step of the journey. It's almost never one single event that leads to success, but rather, a series of small steps-what could be called everyday hustles-that lead to that success. This is why successful people are almost never able to point to one single moment that turned the tide. Instead, the day-to-day grind, working incrementally, moment-by-moment, passionately towards one's dream, is the "magic" that ultimately leads to success.

People don't fail because they don't have worthy dreams; rather, they don't achieve success because they don't want to work on their dreams every moment of every day. They don't want to hustle. If you moan about it every time you have to work on your dream, especially the non-shiny parts, forget it: You've already lost.

I learned early on, that the true key to success in martial arts wasn't showing up once in a while and giving it my all, but rather, being consistent. Even on days I really didn't want to be on the mat, I was there. And when I wasn't on the mat, I was working on things I could change: My attitude; ironing out hang ups that persistently stuck around from childhood, etc.

I realized that true success is a 24/7 job. But not the kind of job you hate. When you are working on something you know will get you where you most want to go, you best be prepared to hustle. You need to put the work in if you want to see those daily successes. The same is true in business.

Sadly, people want "Braveheart" moments, the highs, the applause, the recognition, the lights—but they don't want to go to battle. Being truly successful at anything isn't won in the speech; it's won in the day-to-day battle, in the trenches, where you need to learn to roll with the punches, to accept the bad with the good. Success involves *wabi-sabi,* seeing and accepting that imperfection is part of the process.

Bottom line: If you want success—whether in your martial arts game, in life, or career—you need to be prepared to do the work. No excuses. I'm sorry, as simple as it may sound; there are zero substitutes for hard work. As mentioned earlier, Malcolm Gladwell said that it takes roughly ten-thousand hours of practice to achieve mastery in a field. I spent a decade hustling every single day to achieve the success I have today. Every morning, Monday to Saturday, I woke up at 5:30 AM to be at the gym by 6. I coached private clients all day long, up to ten hours a day, catching a quick nap on the mat between lessons. Why? Because I was passionate about what I did, and I knew it was my ticket out of poverty.

Make sure you are absolutely passionate about your goal, your dream, because if you are not, you simply won't do the daily work required to transform it into a success. Make sure you own it. Too many people live their lives dictated by other people's dreams. When I was growing up, I was told by my mother, and my teachers, that I was wasting my time on martial arts, and that I would never amount to anything. In fact, my religious studies teacher, who had a powerful influence over her students, once told me that nunchucks (chain sticks) were tools of the devil. I never listened. One of my strengths has always been to chart my own path. This doesn't mean I haven't been afraid, or haven't second-guessed myself—I have done plenty of that—but, as I remarked at the beginning of this book, I realized that when things are not exactly perfect is when the good stuff happens.

Working hard however, doesn't mean not working smart. Get a system going. Figure out what is important to making what you want happen. If you are applying the principles presented in this book, break them into smaller chunks, and assign specific times, and days, to work on the different aspects, Even if it means you have to do it at 10 PM. Just do it, even if you don't feel like it.

As I mentioned above, one of the greatest secrets I ever learned about how to achieve peak performance is consistency. Like it or not, that means there will be times when you have to work on your inner game, even when it is simply easier not to. In fact, applying yourself during these times is likely to produce the most rewards. Consistency is far more important than quantity. It's not how much you do, it's how often you do it, and do it well. Doing a small amount of important, quality work every day is far more important to your success than putting in

153

bursts of high-quantity work every once in a while, whenever you "feel like it." Remember: It's the day-to-day hustle that leads to success.

You have to be inspired to hustle. Find people who you admire, who are successful, watch them, listen to them, read their words, and take notes. Then feed those notes into your action performance system. You can be sure that for every success tip I have offered in this book, someone super-successful is using it. Find them and learn from them.

How do I know that? Because I have my heroes, too. I get asked this question a lot: "Do you find inspiration from within the martial arts industry?" My answer is always a resounding: "No!" Seriously, the martial arts industry tends to be consumed by inflated egos and half-baked truths. So I started looking outside my profession for inspiration, for lessons, that I could then translate and apply on the mat. I suggest that everyone else does the same. Don't look within your own industry for answers, look outwards, and you will find no shortage of amazing people who have achieved success despite not having everything perfect. Successful people typically show up with a body attitude that inspires others to listen, to act, and to change.

Then, when you do see success on the horizon, be sure to keep your feet on the ground. Most importantly: *Don't get lazy*! I call it the Rocky Syndrome. In the *Rocky* movies, when Rocky Balboa was hungry, when he was passionate, he ran every day (even when he didn't want to), and he finally succeeded. However, a few movies later, once he had "arrived," with all the trappings of success, he didn't hustle anymore. That was a big mistake. Facing defeat reminded him why he started the journey in the first place: As I quoted Rocky earlier:

"The world ain't all sunshine and rainbows. . . .Ya gotta be willing to take the hits, and not pointing fingers saying you ain't where you wanna be because of him, or her, or anybody! Cowards do that and that ain't you! You're better than that!"

'The World Ain't All Sunshine and Rainbows'

I have always been a pragmatist. I don't believe in luck. Luck is for someone who doesn't have a plan. I also know life is tough, and will kick you between the legs if given half a chance. Taking a risk, putting yourself on the line to become more, can be a scary proposition.

Central to my success over the years has been my ability to be creative and innovative. I have always been really good at thinking outside the box. Even writing this book is pushing the envelope and going against the status quo in a world of modern martial arts - which is fixated more on fighting than living. I'm very aware that suggesting modern martial arts can be a catalyst for personal transformation, and not just a way to beat someone in a cage, is not popular. It takes guts, and a thick skin to go against the grain. And yes, going against the grain can bring up fear. But fear is only our enemy if we let it stop us.

No doubt, it's going to be scary at times applying the principles in this book. Much of what I have written here is not how most people aim for peak performance. I know this because my clients tell me so all the time. However, once they taste success, they are forever transformed. As I tell them: "Imagine if every single one of us were taught from day one in school, how best to manage negative emotions, or be mindful?" Schools teach us a lot—except the most important and crucial thing: How to successfully live in an unpredictable, crazy, upside-down world.

Most people are scared, and don't even know it. I see this in my own field. People line up in droves to take up self-defense lessons, or mixed martial arts (MMA) training. Ironically, most will likely never be attacked, and even fewer will ever get in a cage to compete. What's more, most MMA schools are located in upper-middle class, affluent neighborhoods - a far cry from the violent streets of Brazilian favelas, or townships in South Africa, or gang-infested areas of inner cities. What's really going on? In short: Worldwide, people have a need for inner security, something most of us have never been taught how to achieve. Ironically, affluence seems to make more and more people insecure—because affluence takes us away from ourselves.

Coming home to oneself takes inner creativity and some innovative ideas—but it is also likely to be scary. It almost always involves taking some risks, and overcoming fears. How, then, do you take risk? How do you overcome fear? My answer is quite simple and straightforward. In fact, it's so simple; you might well think I'm bonkers: You need to play more. That's it: *You need to play more!*

Some risk is inherent in creativity and innovation. In my experience, people often talk about "creativity" and "innovation," as elements for gaining a competitive advantage; but, little or no discussion focuses on the real reason it is so difficult to implement. The problem is that most people are risk averse (blame evolution here). Taking risks triggers consequences, and, while some of these consequences are real, most are often imagined. But, real or imagined, the risk of failure, or pain, holds many people back from achieving the kind of success they say they want.

Nowhere is this more evident than in sparring. When someone is throwing punches at your face, coming up with creative solutions can be a scary proposition. Should you fail, the consequence, of course, is, well . . . you get punched in the face. Most people simply try to cover and survive, or worse, try a repeated failed strategy over and over, in hopes of getting a different result.

However, in order to deal with someone throwing punches at your face, you have to be creative with your approach, think of new ways of moving to meet the challenge, and then, have the confidence to put these embodied ideas into practice. Again, so many people have a hard time with this because of their fear of taking risk. Sparring, like life, can often be chaos in action—you have no idea what your opponent is going to do in the next moment (more than likely, he or she doesn't know either). You have to react to rapidly changing circumstances, be adaptable, and yes, come up with creative solutions in the moment. You need to innovate them into existence, all while someone is trying to hurt you. I have seen strong, skilled, and talented people completely freeze in these moments.

Naturally, anyone taking up martial arts would like to improve their performance. But, if they choke every time they face a decisive hit-or-be-hit moment, eventually they will give up. As a coach, I tackled the fear of risk head on. No one is going to be creative if the consequence of taking risk is too high. For example, when clients step on the mat with me to spar, they take some risk whenever they try something new. But if I punch them so hard I knock them out, they will simply refuse to ever try anything new again. That kind of experience shuts down a person's willingness to think outside the box—because the consequences of being creative were just too high.

However, let's say I challenge you just above your comfort zone- but in a playful way- where you know that I am simply trying to tag you with a punch, and not knock you out, you will then be more inclined to take risk, and when you do take that risk, creativity and innovation become natural byproducts.

Experience has taught me that, given the opportunity, people are naturally creative. Sadly, most of us lose this innate capacity once we grow up (watch Sir Ken Robinson's TED Talk on "Why Schools Kill Creativity"). Fear holds us back. Fear of failure. Fear of looking bad. Fear of the consequences.

If you want to be creative, first you have to remove the type of risk that could stop you from ever playing again.

Over the years, I have developed a model that inspires creativity and innovation on the mat (it works equally well in other organizations, too). Both I, and many of my clients, have used this model to great effect, on and off the mat. The main elements of the model are:

1. *Creativity involves risk.* Recognize and accept that some risk is built into creativity and innovation. In fact, I would argue that without risk, creativity and innovation no longer exist.

2. *Encourage risk, minimize consequences.* In order for people to take risk, their environment must not only encourage creativity, but should be such that the consequences, or payback, of taking that risk shouldn't be so high that a person would never come back and try again.

3. *Shift from competition to play.* Facilitating risk requires a shift in mindset, from competition to playful challenge. In competition, one person, or team, has to lose in order for another to win. In a challenge-play environment, people are

encouraged to shift from playing *within* boundaries (i.e. rules of winning) to playing *with* the boundaries (i.e. finding ways to continue to play). Bottom line: The seriousness of loss needs to be removed, along with the focus on winning, not looking bad, or the fear of making mistakes. It is much better to cultivate a sense of play.

4. ***Allow for failure and learn from mistakes.*** With a focus on *play,* people no longer seek to dominate others with power, and they instead learn to enjoy playing with strength. One of the main reasons people fail is because they are never *allowed* to fail. As pointed out earlier, if the consequences of failing are too high, many people often won't even try. By not trying, by not engaging in the challenges of life, they hope to avoid failure. But giving up before you even begin is itself, already a form of failure. If you cannot fail, then you can never explore your full potential, because, you are simply too afraid. In my experience, environments that don't allow people to fail encourage the mindset of the tough, the alpha males, and the bullies. Unfortunately, this outmoded way of being, continues to dominate the world of many modern organizations.

5. ***Balance risk with play.*** Playing is an antidote to the severe consequences of taking risk. Taking risk shouldn't be about keeping score, or time; rather, it should be about finding ways to more effectively improve your game, and expand your sense of time. It should be an experience that anyone, regardless of experience or status, should be able to engage in.

In a play-risk environment, chances are you will meet someone with better skills or greater strength, someone who can playfully provide the challenge necessary for you to grow and develop. In play, winning and losing take on a different definition. Rather than "winning" or "losing" marking the end of the game, they are simply seen as moments in the ongoing process of play itself. In play, the ultimate objective is not for the game to end, but for the game to continue.[16]

As entrepreneur and blogger Seth Godin put it, this is the essence of creating *art*. Art results from the successful implementation of creativity and innovation.

Even more important, playful challenge creates resilience. Resilience increases as your confidence to take risks begins to pay off in creative and innovative solutions. You then naturally want to hustle, work hard, and move in the direction of your dreams. Without these ingredients, you will not have any real opportunities for resilience to develop. Couple this play-risk approach with the tools already outlined in this book, and you will increase your chance of bouncing back from setbacks. You learn to bounce where others freeze.

---

[16] See *Finite and Infinite Games* by James Carse for more on this distinction.

The Meta-Principle of Success

Become an IGAMER

And so we near the end of this book. I hope you have enjoyed reading it. More important, though, I hope you have gotten something valuable out of it. In this final chapter, I will outline my "IGAMER" method, an easy way to remember, in six quick principles, what I have covered in this book.

First, as noted in the opening chapters, ever since seventeenth-century French philosopher René Descartes separated the mind from what the body does. Western societies have been conditioned to the idea that mind and body are separate and function independently of each other. As a result, as body-mind psychotherapist Susan Aposhyan noted in, *Natural Intelligence: Body-Mind Integration and Human Development*, for centuries the Western scientific paradigm has reduced the human body to a machine, ignoring the fact that every body, every organism, tingles with feelings and experiences. But we are not machines made of meat. We are *sentient embodied organisms* that use our minds to direct how and when our bodies move. Our "meat" throbs with the vitality of feelings and sensations, tingles with emotions, and sparkles with thoughts and volition . . . how different from any mere machine! This is what science has overlooked, ever since it embraced the mind-body split.

Thankfully, things are changing: The mind-body split is being exposed as the myth it always was. Hopefully, even in some small way, this book adds to the growing trend to re-integrate mind and body. The underlying premise of my life, and work, is the principle that *who we are on the inside,* determines success more than what we do or even what we know.

The felt relationship to our body is a precondition for successful performance—whether your goal is to simply "up" your martial arts game, or, more ambitiously, to take on life and succeed. However, to achieve this, you need to practice and develop in-the-moment awareness of whatever is happening in your body (sensations, movements, attitude, etc.), as well as in your mind (thoughts, emotions, values, goals, etc.). While logic, rationality, and fact-gathering are important, too many people focus on these objective factors to the exclusion of their rich inner, subjective world.

Develop your 'IGAME'

Full-Contact Living is about bringing your embodied, subjective "GAME" back into your life and work. Think of it as "personal-growth hacking" for peak performance—but with an embodied twist. To help you remember how to achieve this, I came up with an acronym that summarizes the key tools presented in this book. I call it the "IGAMER method." Let me explain . . .

'I' for Imperfection.

Imperfection creates opportunities for success. Just because things are not perfect, doesn't mean you should do nothing. Rather, get in there; take action, even if you don't have all the answers yet. Success happens on the journey, in the day-to-day grind, in the little things, which we often take for granted. Take note of how you interact with the small things in your life—because, taken together, they shape who you will become.

'G' for Grounded Thinking.

Thinking isn't bad, but what you focus on can be. Reflecting on past mistakes, and planning for the future, are crucial to long-term achievement, but when it comes to performance in the moment, where it matters most, past and future can get you into trouble. When your thoughts move into the past or the future, you can easily get caught up in a mental vortex and spin out of control. Most important, you lose contact with the present moment, the only moment when you can fully respond with clarity.

Remember to apply your re-focus strategies, anchors, in-between and pre-performance routines, to help ground your thinking in the present moment. Peak performance always happens *now*, and grounding your mind in your body, is one of the most effective techniques for returning attention to the present moment.

'A' for Attitude Embodied.

How you show up in the world matters more than you might think. Bottom line: While our minds and bodies are different, they always go together. That's why it is crucial for professionals to develop a keener sense of what I call their "mind-body interface." To be poised for real success, we must understand, and experience, how what goes on in our minds impacts what goes on with our bodies, and vice versa. The way you hold your body—the body attitude you display—will not only change how you feel about yourself, but how others perceive you. Better yet, it tells your mind that you are confident.

'M' for Mindfulness-in-Action.

Mindfulness is a state of being where you are able to just *be present* without judging the outcome of your performance. It involves not becoming attached to the way you are thinking, or attaching to whatever sensations arise in your body, as well as how you define or interpret your sensations to produce your emotions. Mindfulness gives you the ability to be fully present, which then leads to having a "fluid mind." Mindfulness is crucial when dealing with difficult emotions. If you can stay present when someone is throwing a punch at your face, or when faced with difficult situations at work — achieving that quality of presence in all aspects of your life becomes so much easier.

'E' for Exhale.

Breathing isn't just something you do to stay alive; equally important, you need to breathe in order to act. Correct breathing—especially a focus on the out-breath—brings about autonomic nervous system balance, correcting sympathetic over-activity, and parasympathetic under activity, and their consequences: Including internal tension, anxiety, and a myriad of other psycho-physiological health challenges that result from this imbalance.

Learning how to breathe, in ways that trigger the parasympathetic nervous system (responsible for calming the mind-body), is crucial to peak performance in high pressure situations, where, too often, we simply forget to breathe. Furthermore, focusing on our out-breath is the fastest way to get back to the present moment.

And there you have it: The IGAMER method. To help you remember what the acronym stands for, I suggest you print out these six simple sentences (they capture the essence of this book and what you need for successful *full-contact living:*

- I—Accept Impermanence and Imperfection *(wabi-sabi).*
- G—Ground your thoughts in what matters now (embodied mind).
- A—Change the Attitude of your body to show up with presence (mind-body integration)
- M—Be Mindful in the midst of chaos (cultivate mind-body awareness),

- E—Exhale to keep calm and present-focused (breathe your nervous system).

- R—Finally, apply these five IGAME principles to become Resilient, to bounce back with confidence as an IGAMER.

Now it's up to you to practice and apply the six IGAMER principles as your passport to success in *full-contact living*.

About The Author

Rodney is a Doctoral student at the University of Leicester's School of Management. His research area of interest is in the inner management of leaders, with a specific attention to its embodied nature, and the influence of mindfulness-in-action to this process. He earned a masters degree in Leading Innovation and Change. In addition he is a certified Executive Coach, and Registered Somatic Movement Educa-

tor. He created two martial art lifestyle brands (Crazy Monkey Defense and Monkey-Jits) that are now taught in over 15-countries around the world.

In the past two decades he has worked with Army Special Forces on developing high-performance mindsets during intense engagement. He has instructed law enforcement officers both in the United State, Canada and Germany on how to protect themselves when all else fails. He has worked closely with corporate executives, emerging leaders and CEOs to access their inner game and gain the winning edge both mentally and emotionally to enhance their careers.

Brought up on the tough streets of the South Side of Johannesburg, in government housing (similar to the Projects in the USA), he learned early on that the key to surviving any situation comes down to how well you are able to manage your inner game. This has become his life's work. You can think of Rodney as an inner-management fitness coach, where he coaches his clients how to harness the natural intelligence of their mind and body.

You can contact Rodney about his programs, coaching and seminars at his website: www.coachrodneyking.com

Notes

Notes

Notes

10148607R00096

Printed in Great Britain
by Amazon.co.uk, Ltd.,
Marston Gate.